Ethereal Flowers

A Unique Coloring Book for Adults

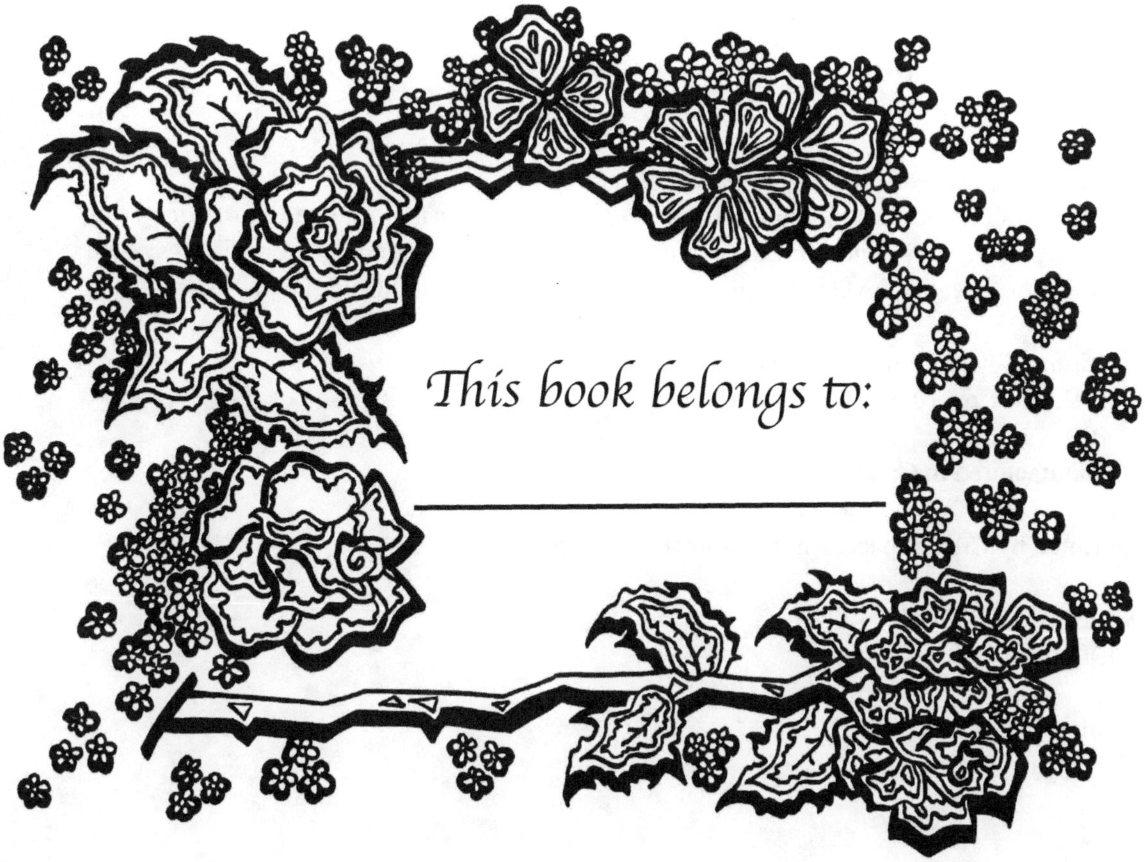

This book belongs to:

_____

40 Hand-Drawn Designs by Olivia Schiopu

Ethereal Flowers : A Unique Coloring Book for Adults

Original Illustrations by Olivia Schiopu
Book and Cover Design by Ioana Schiopu

Manufactured in Canada

Printed by CreateSpace, An Amazon.com Company

ISBN-13: 978-1530712243
ISBN-10: 1530712246

coloring@riosart.net
www.riosart.net

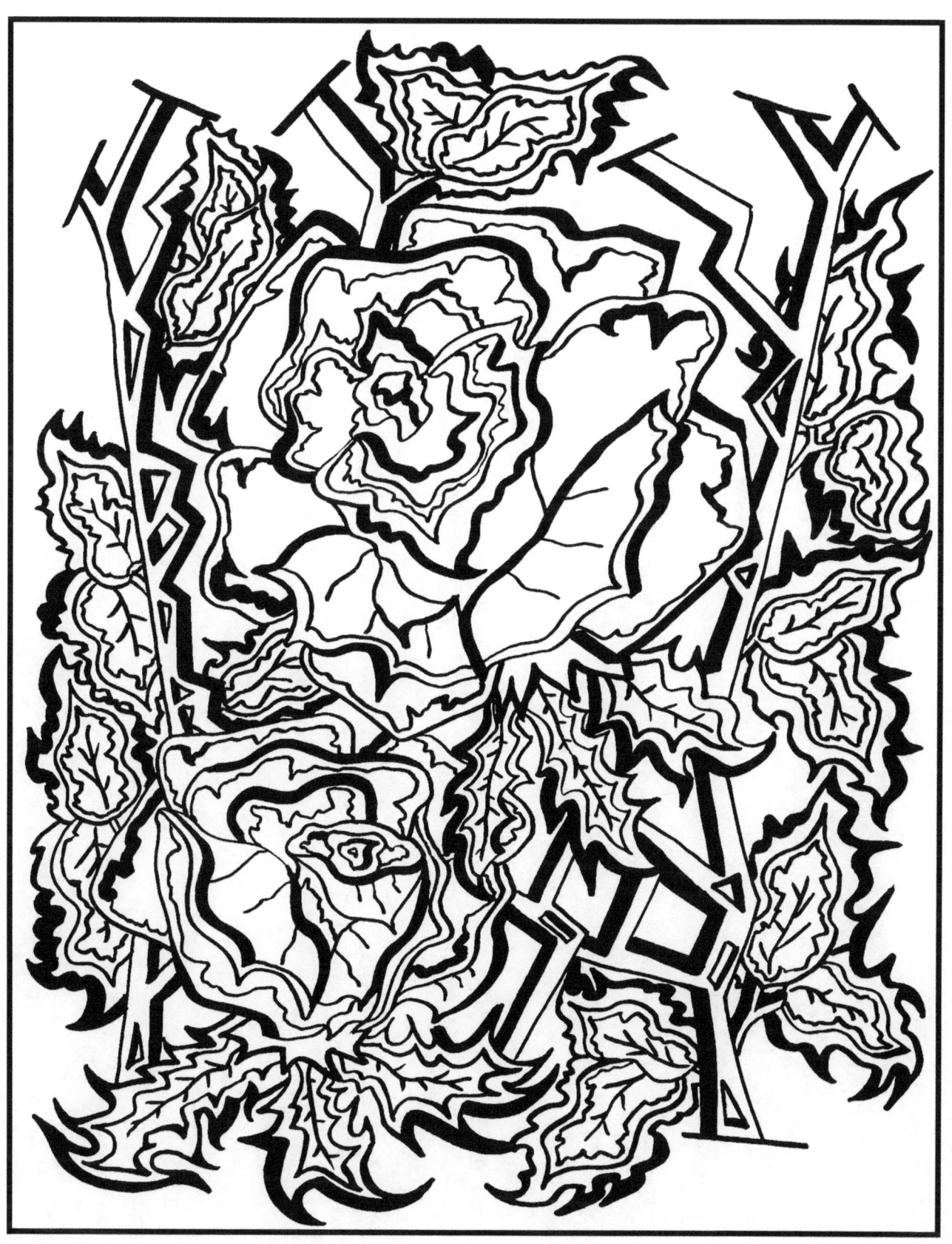

1

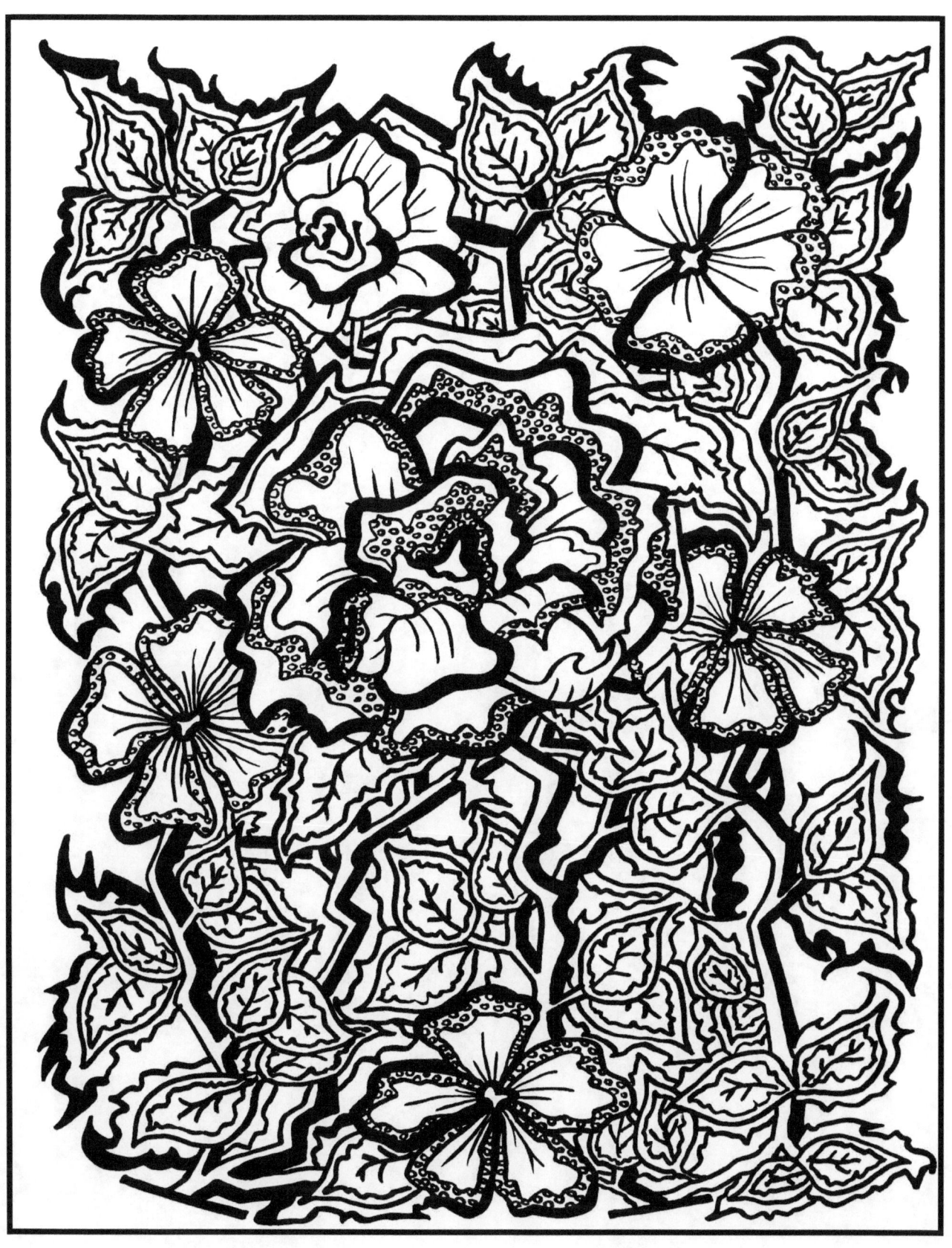

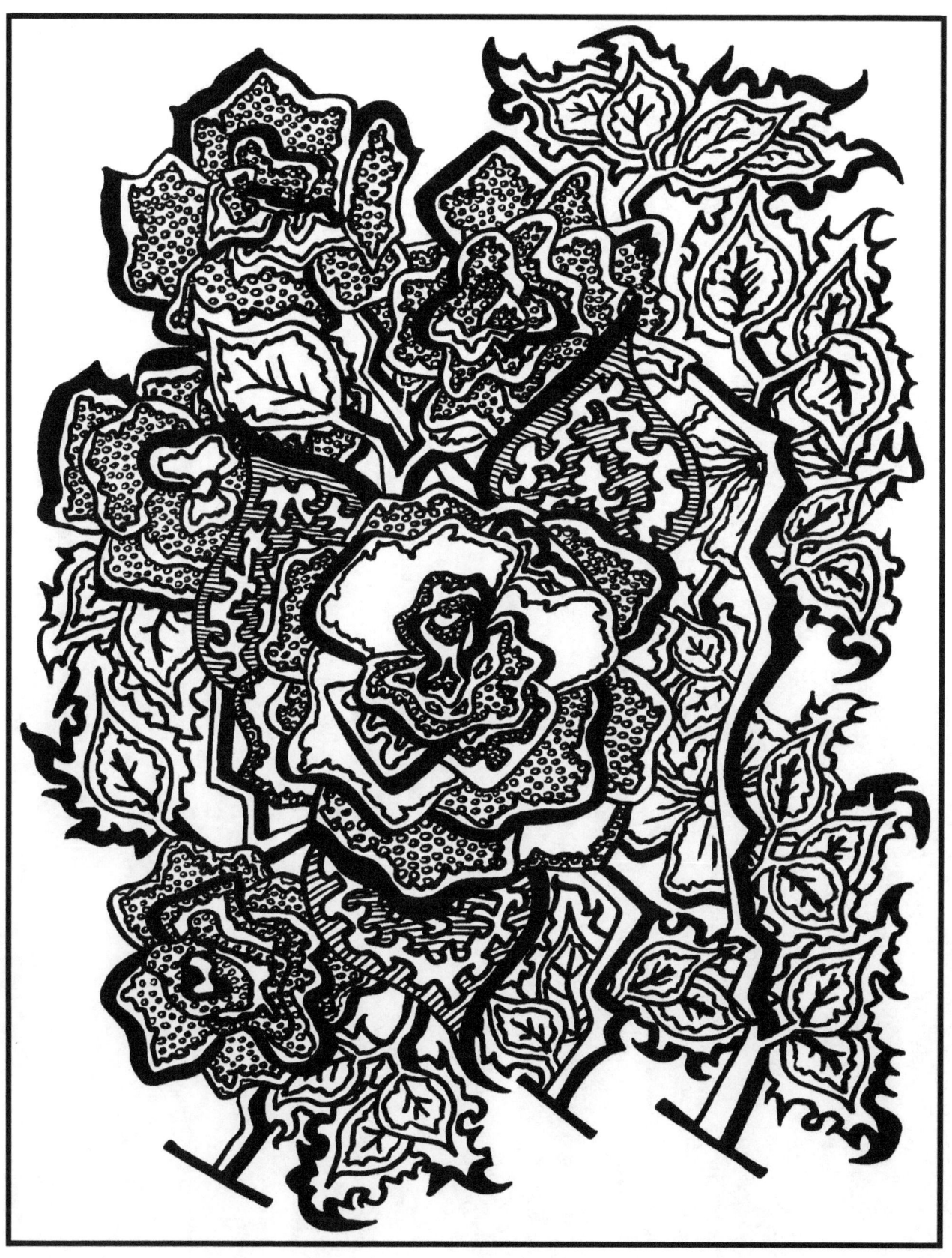

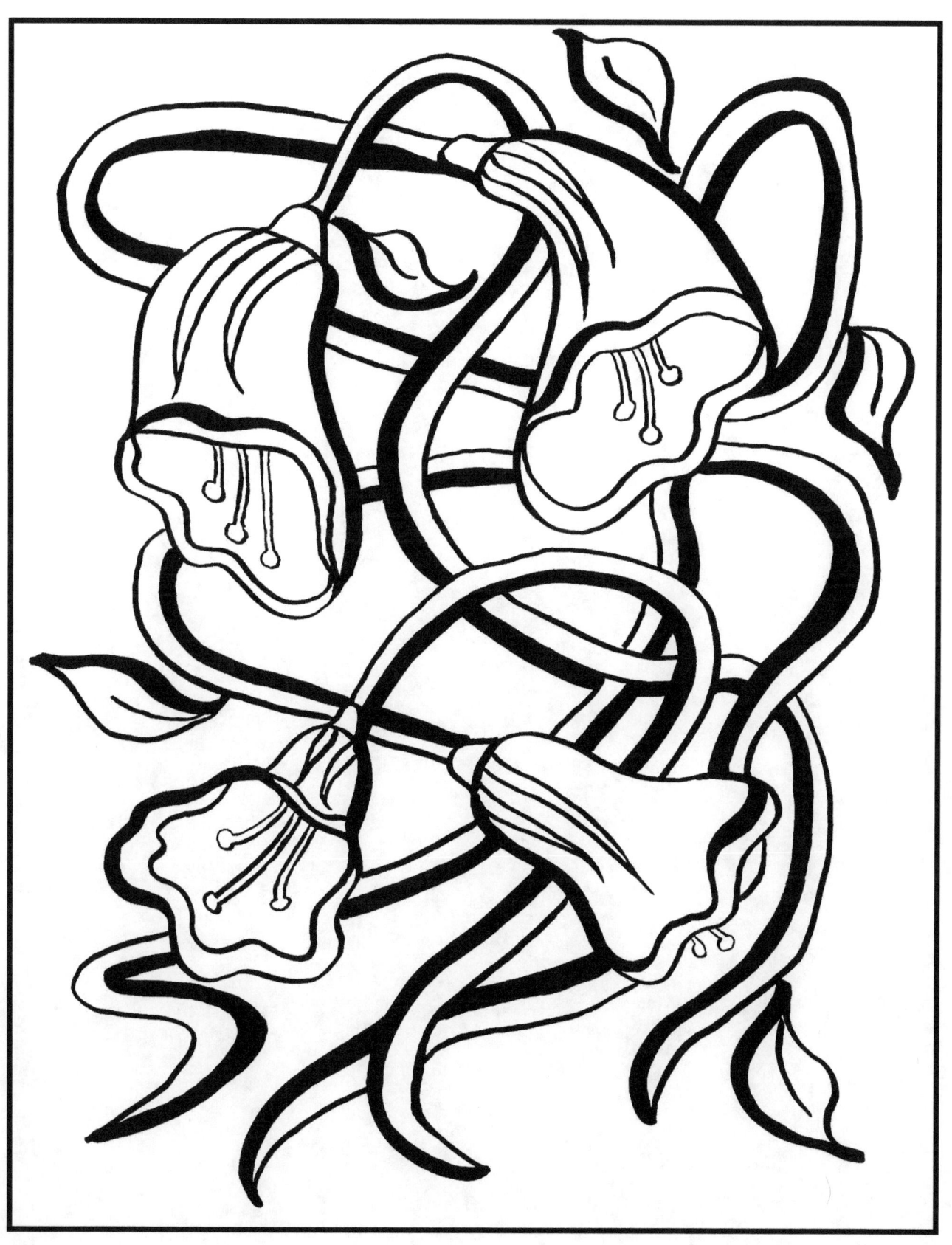

4

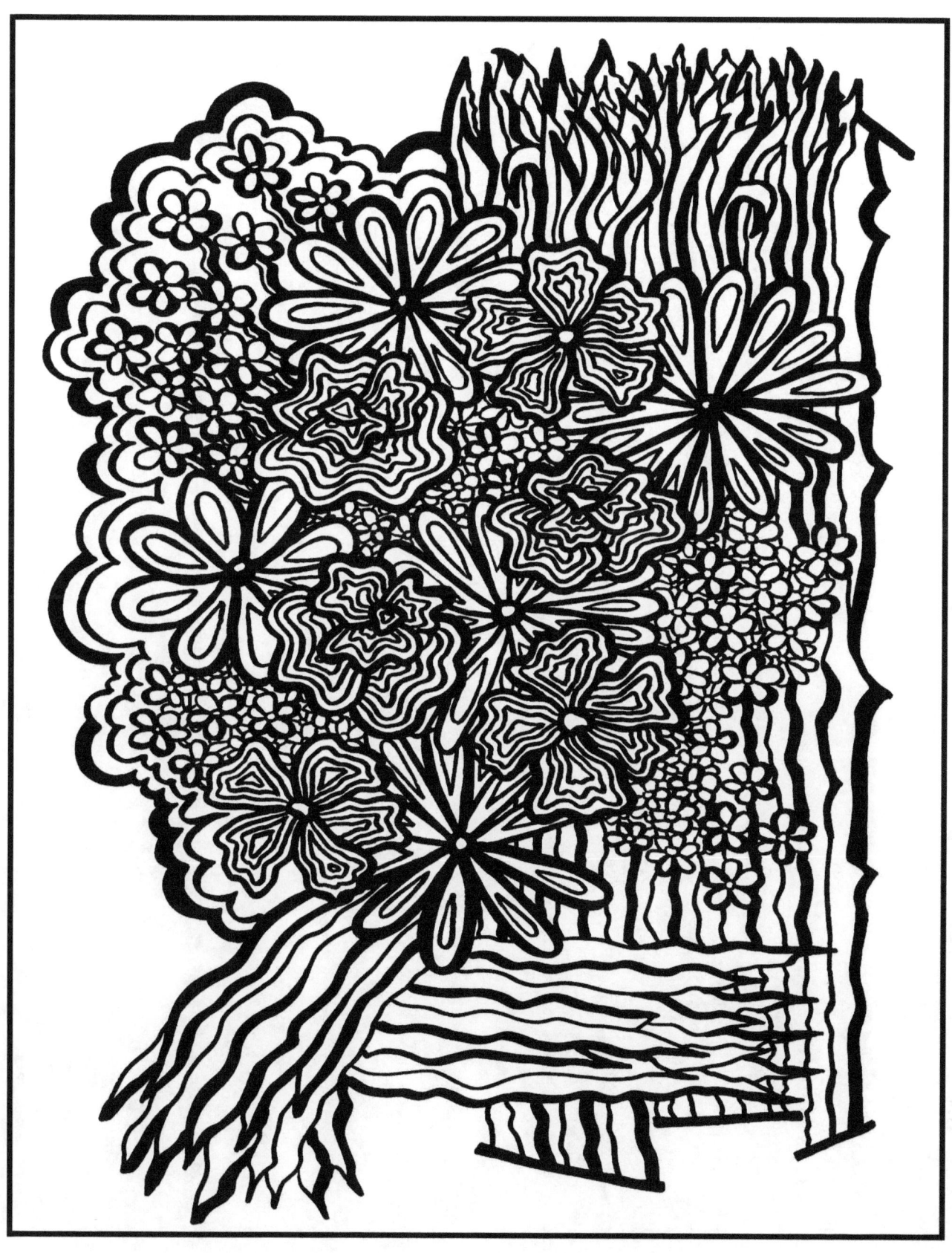

5

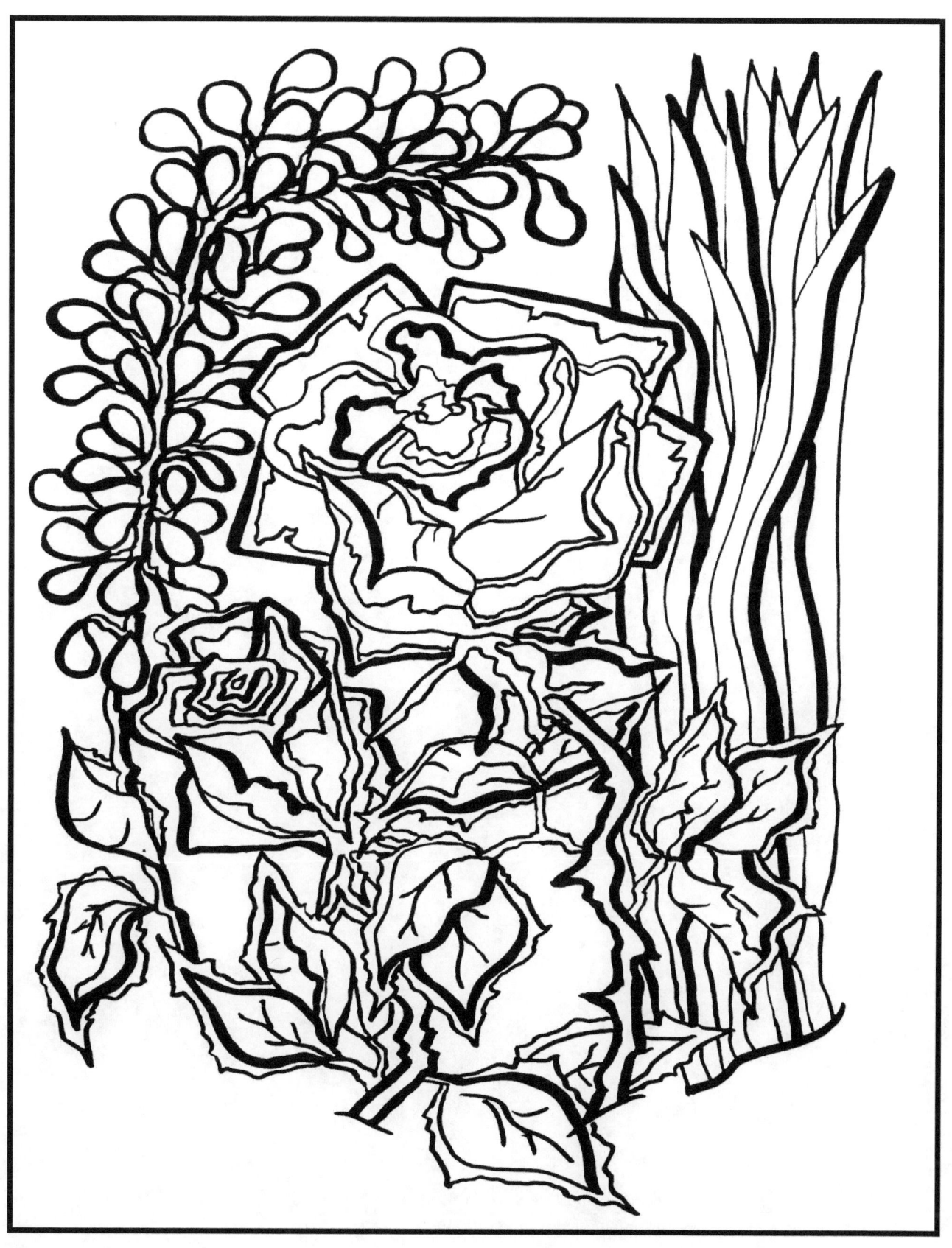

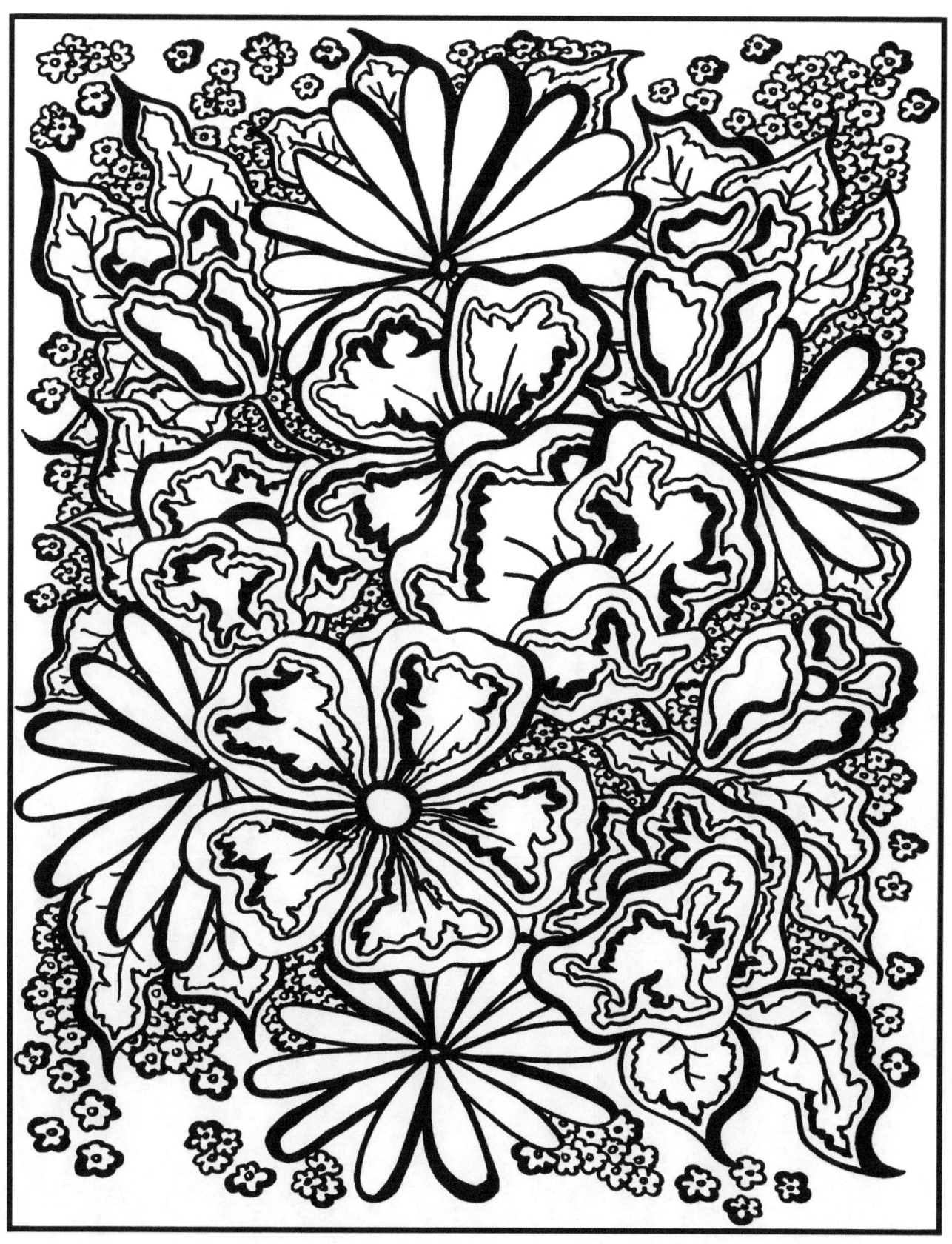

7

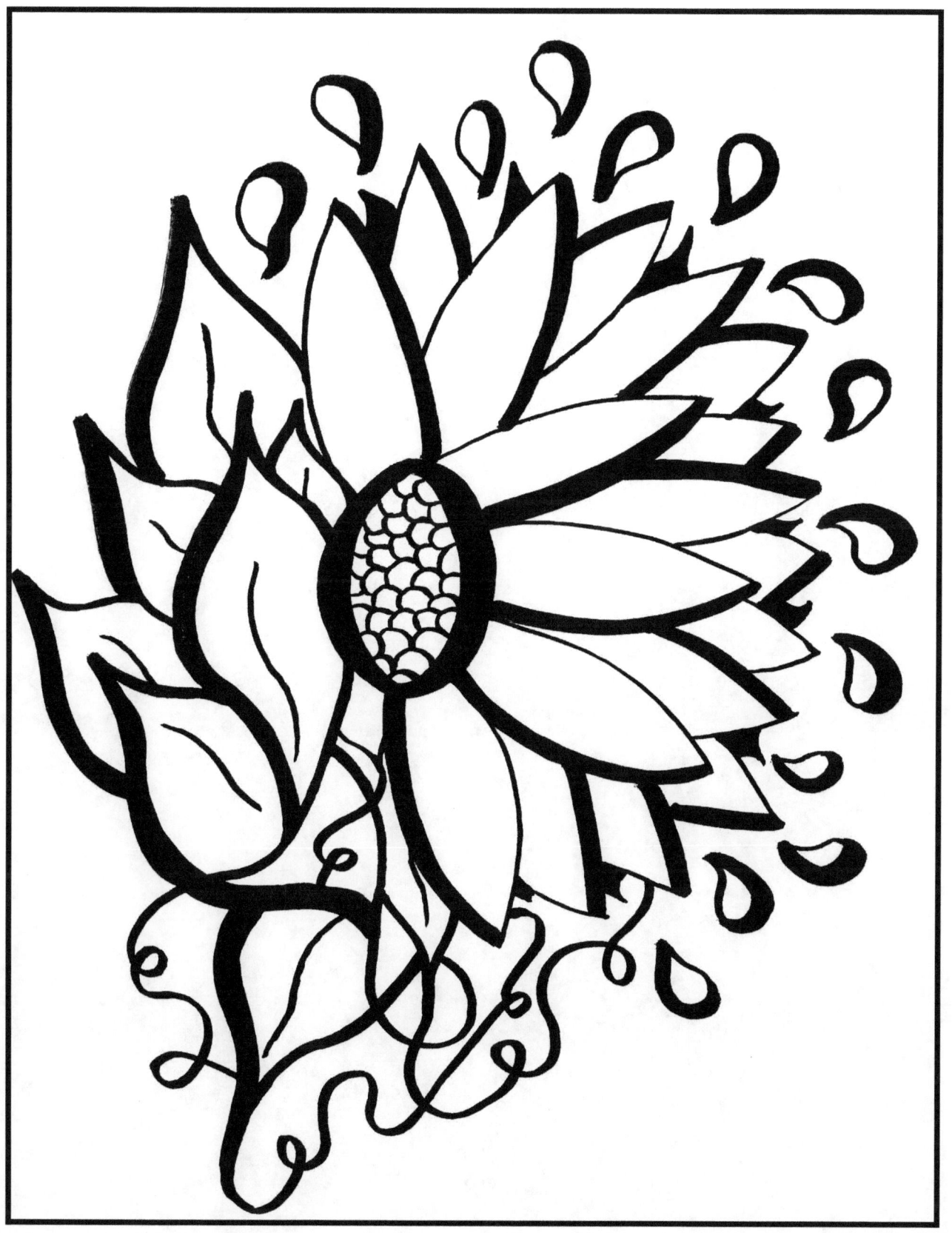

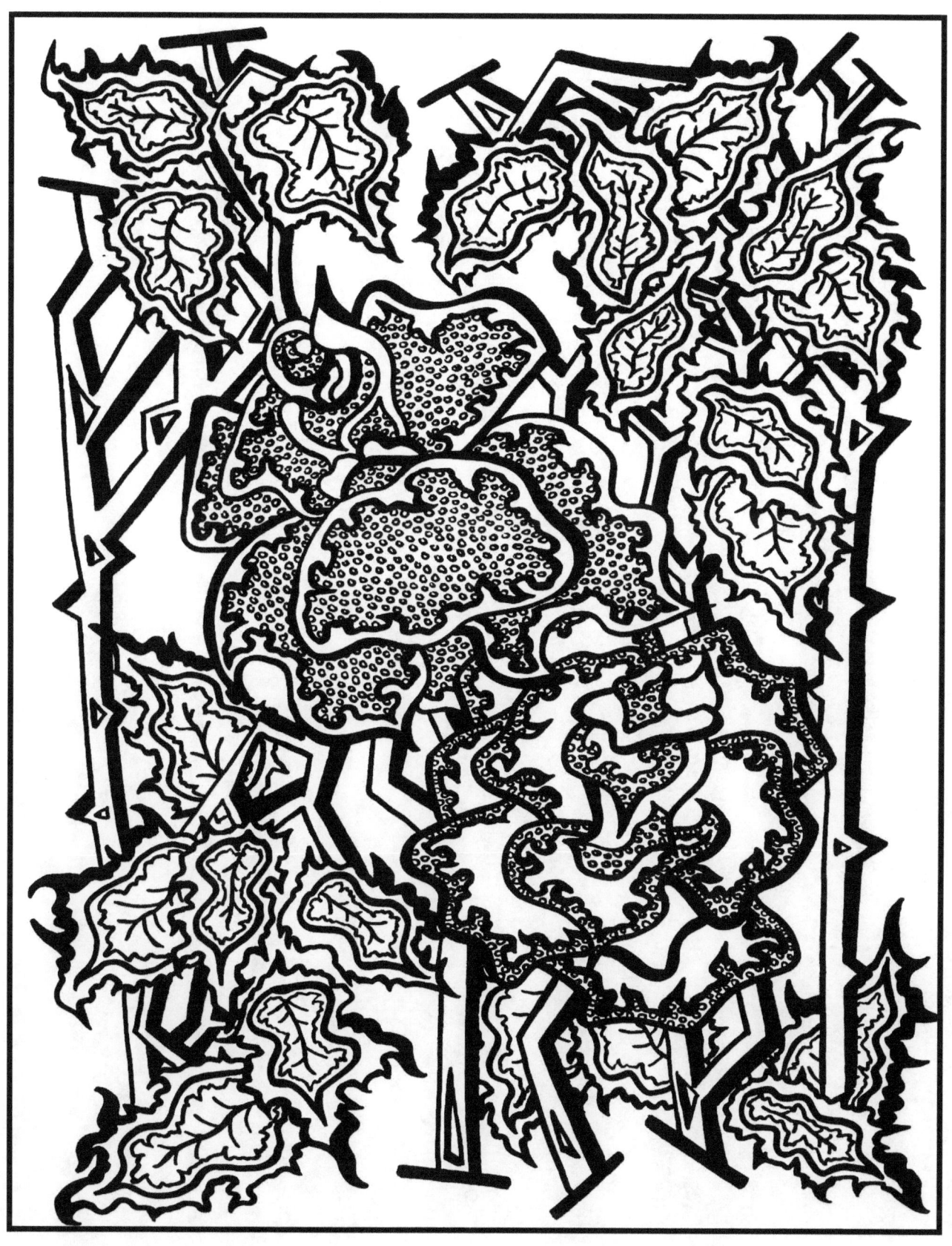

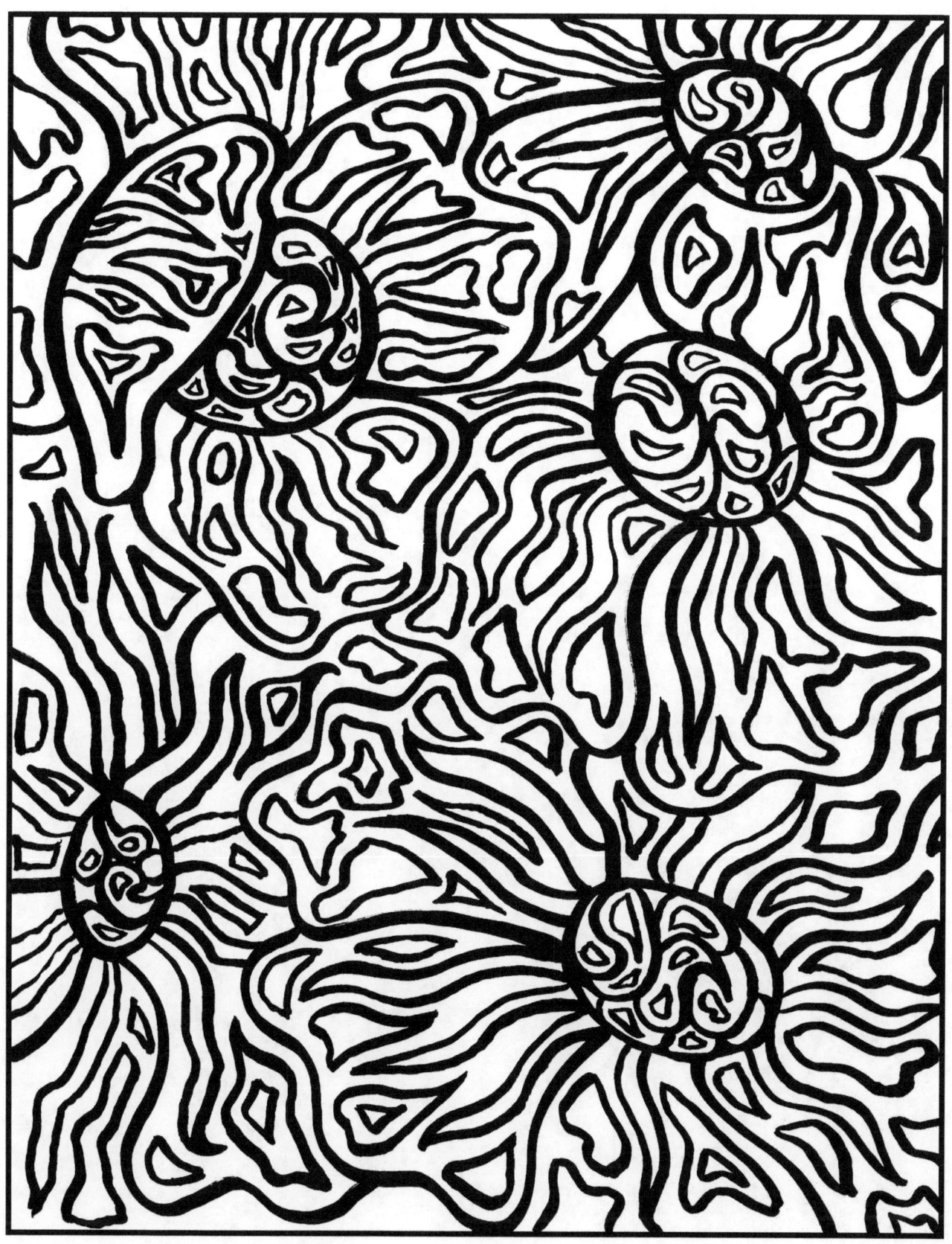

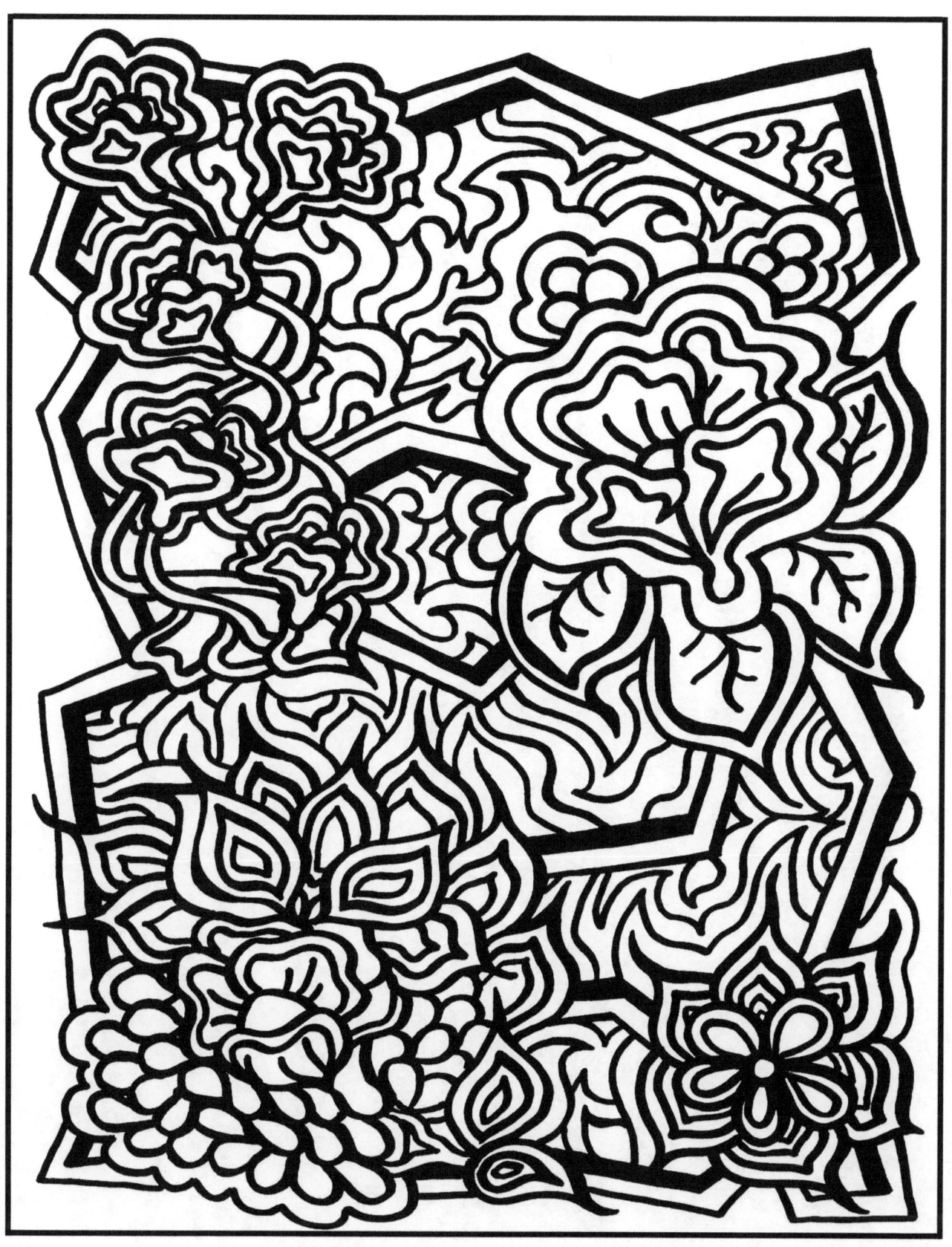

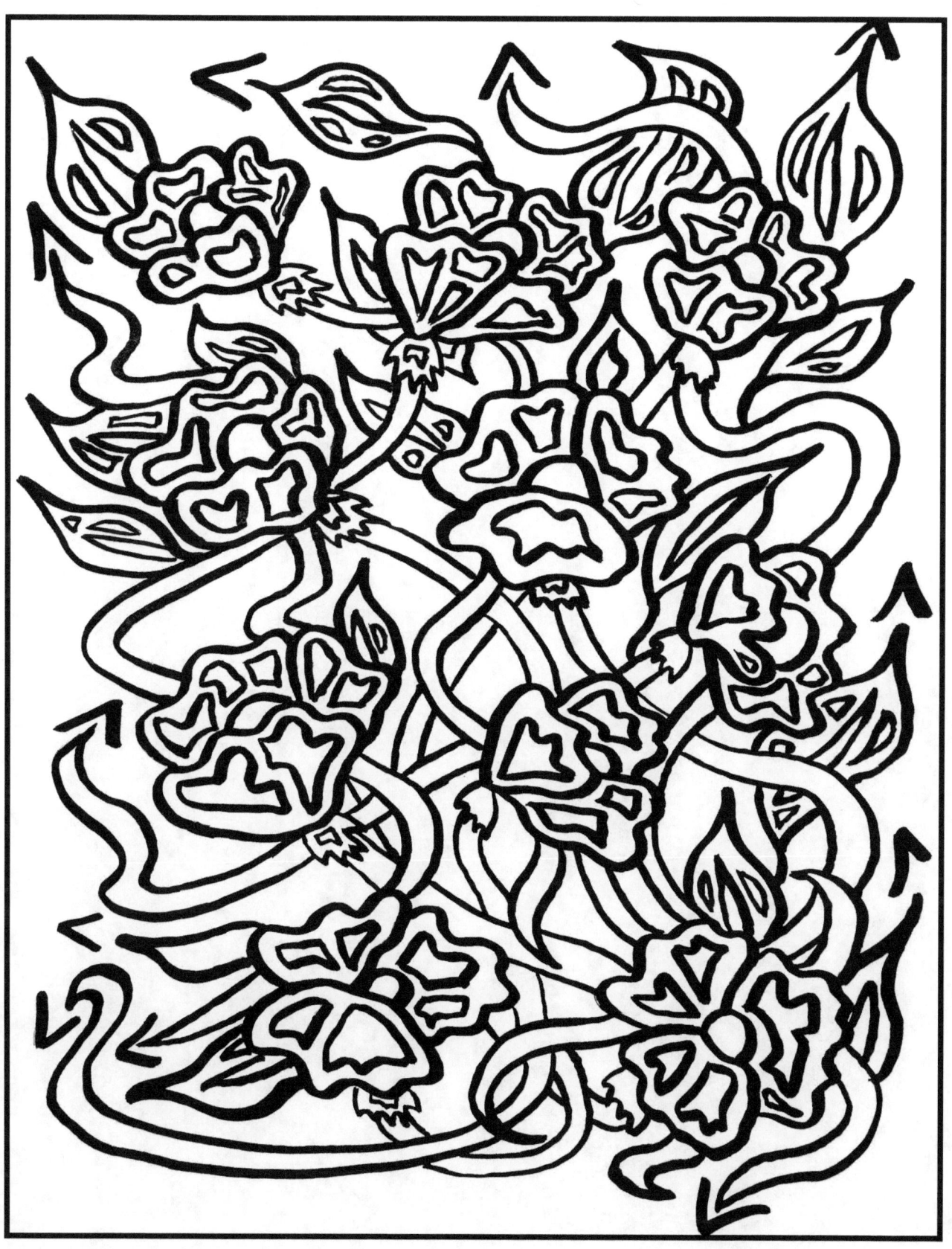

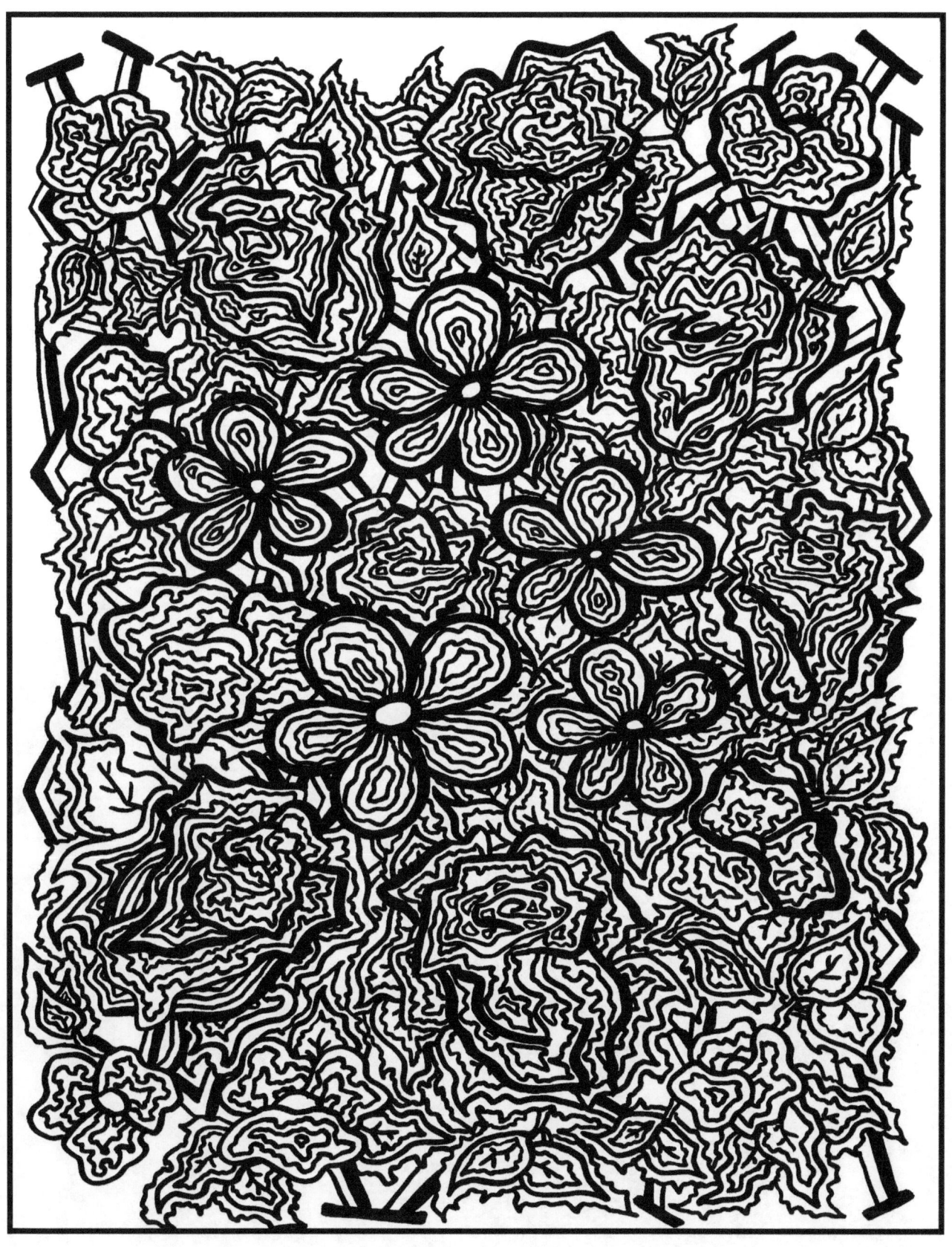

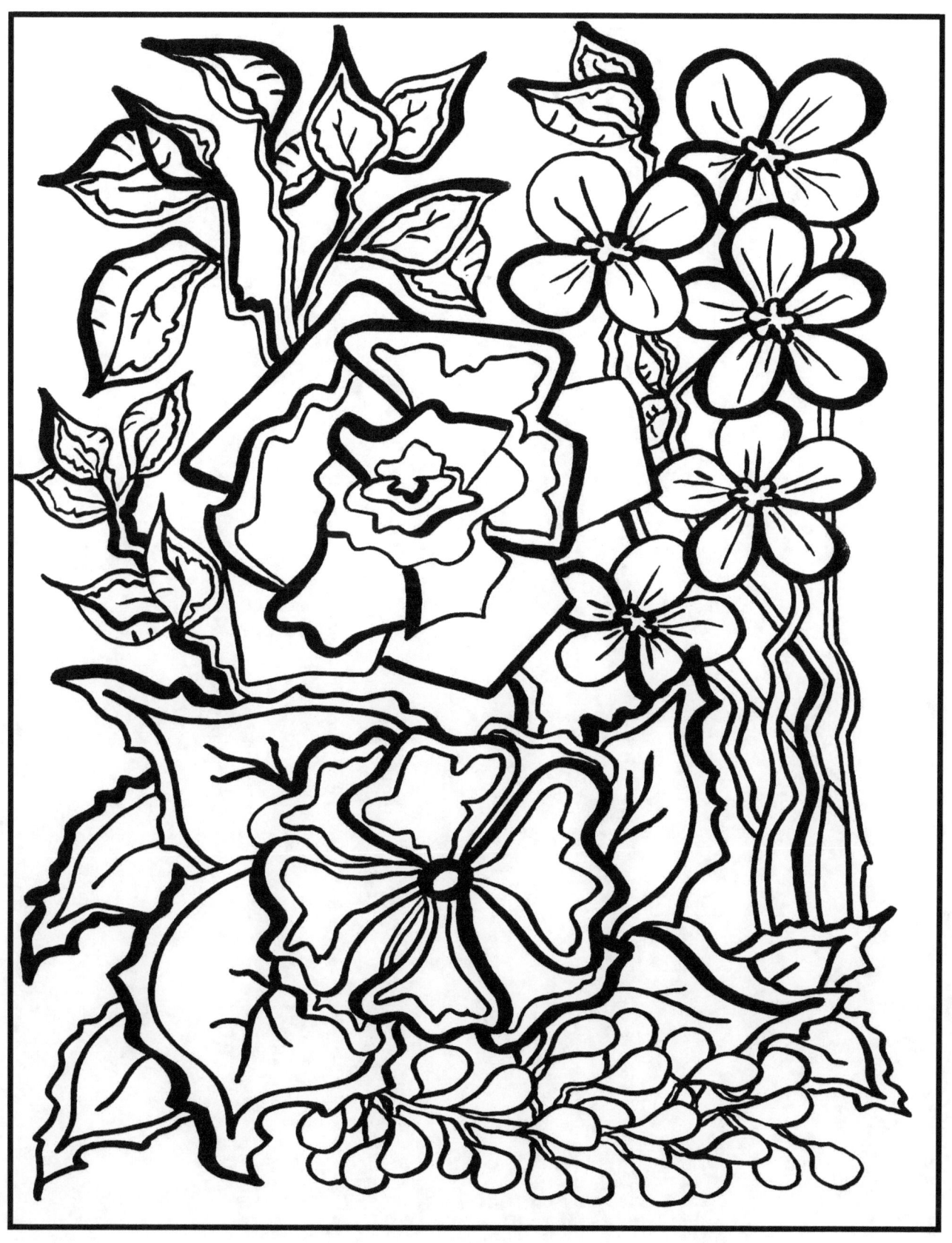

14

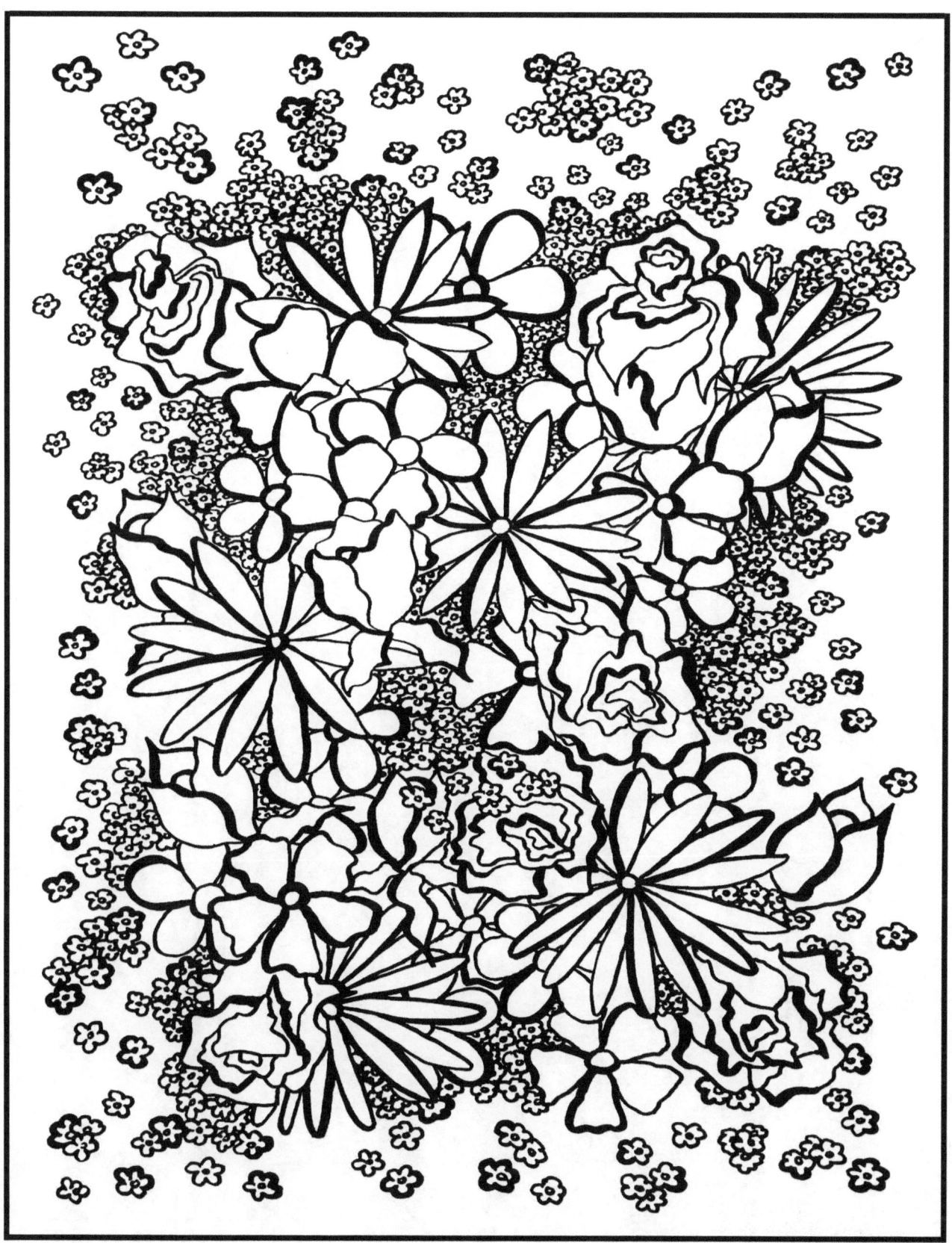

15

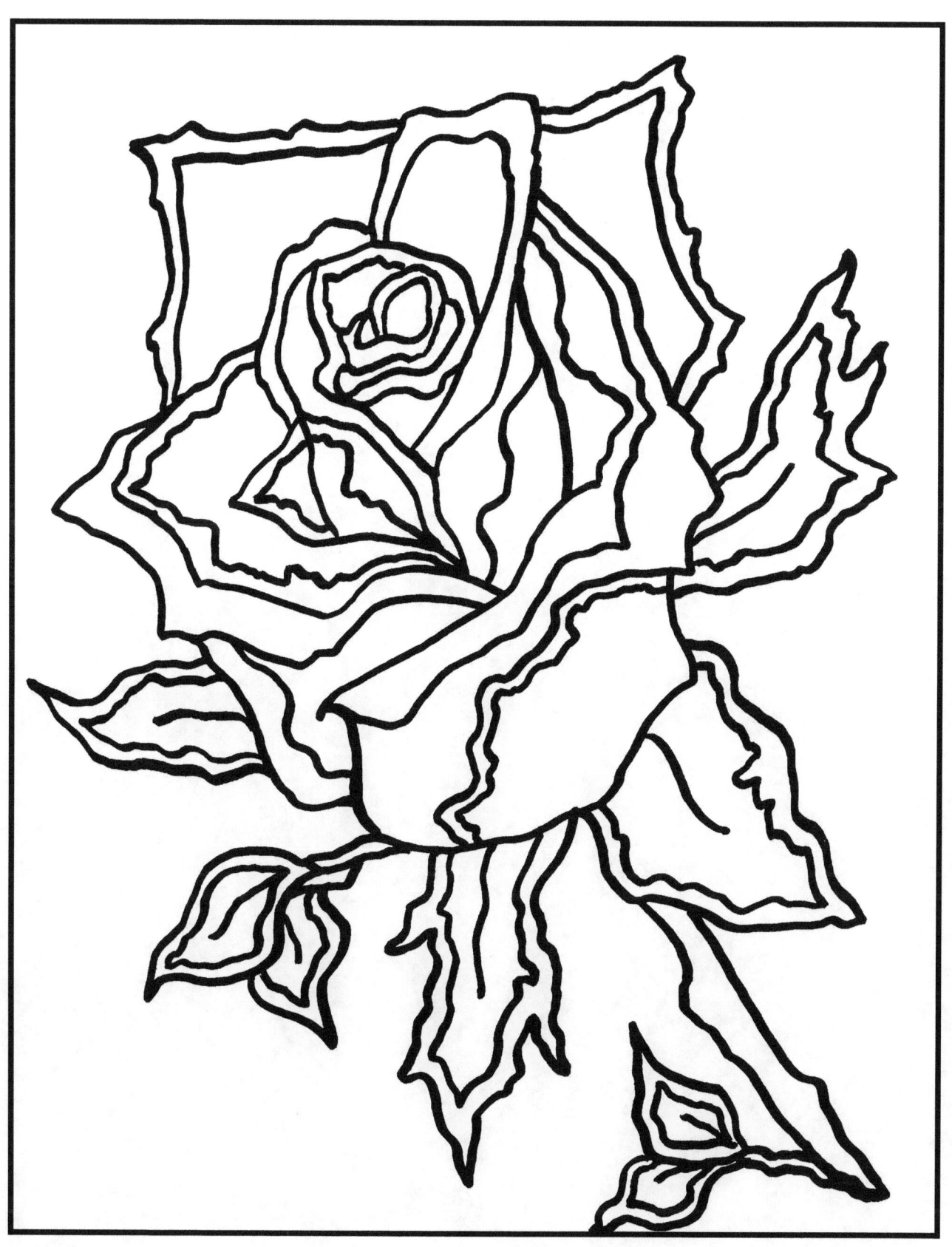

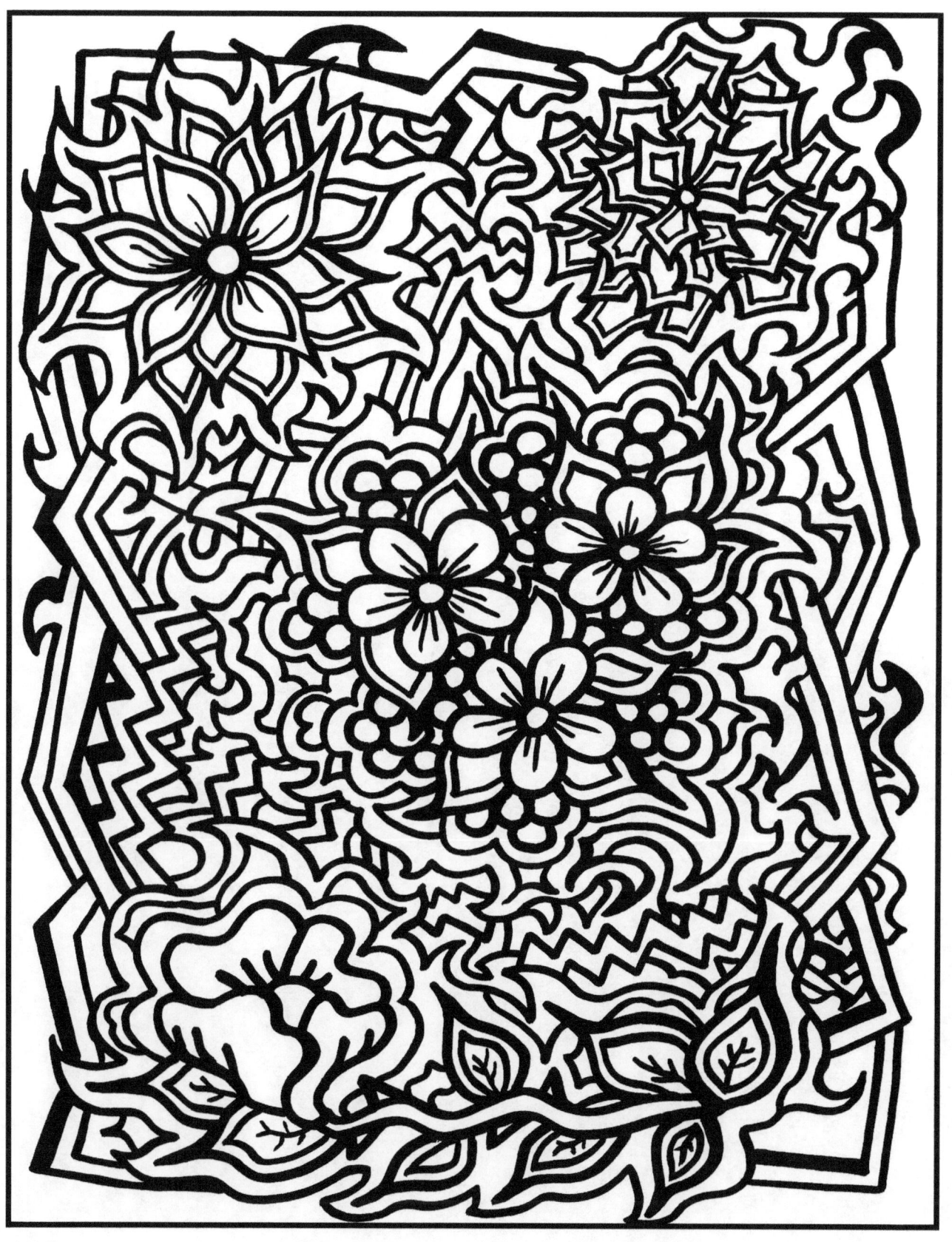

17

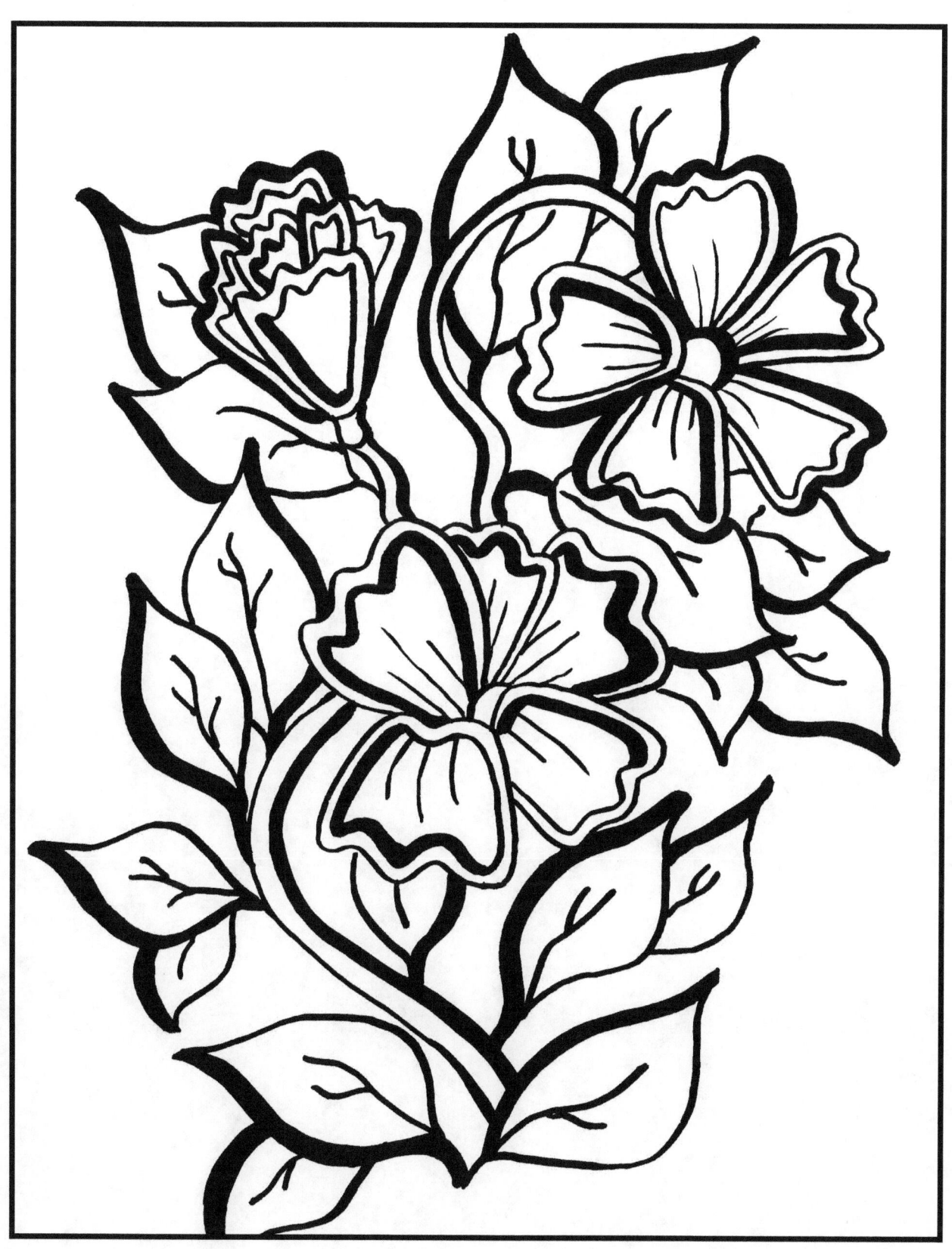

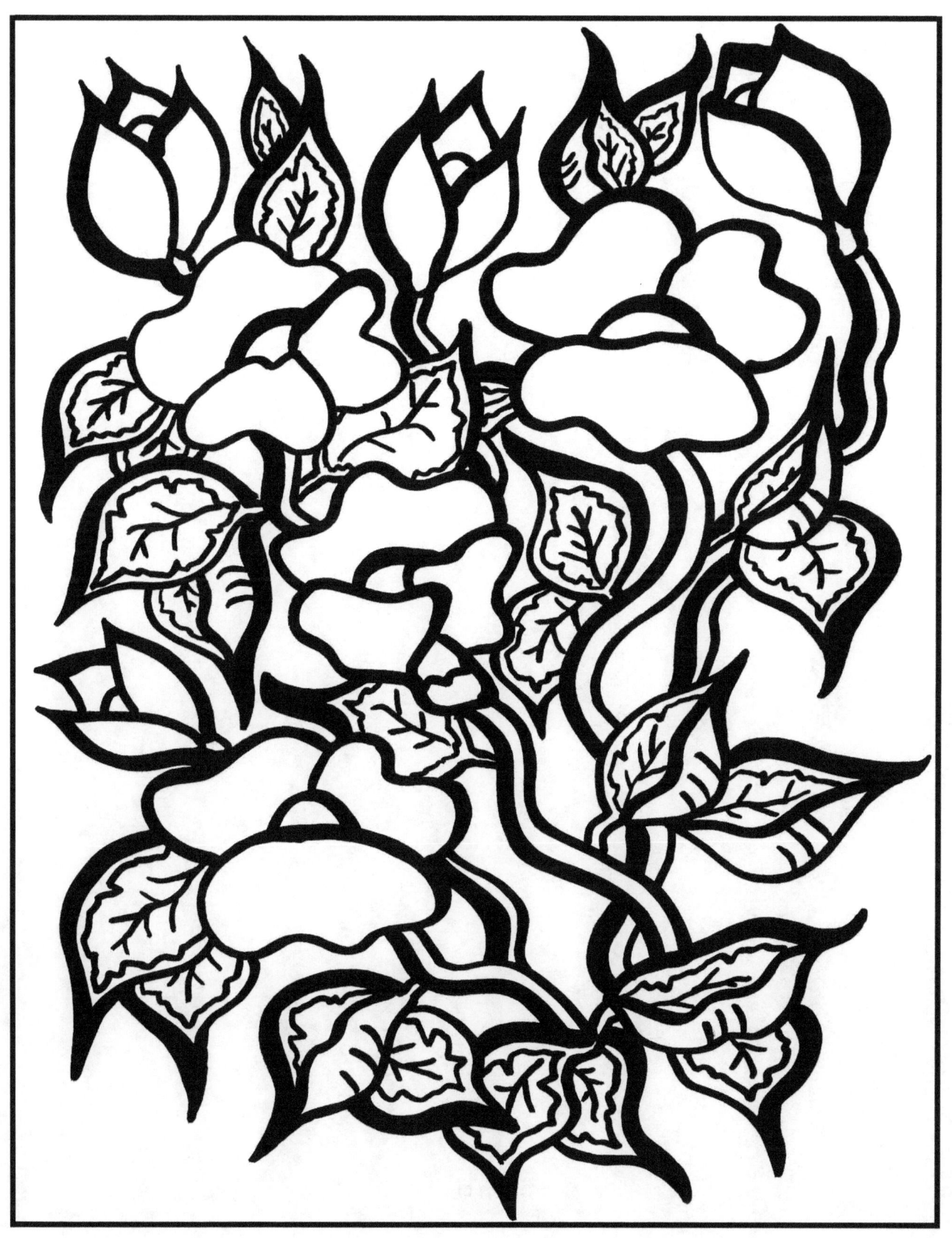

19

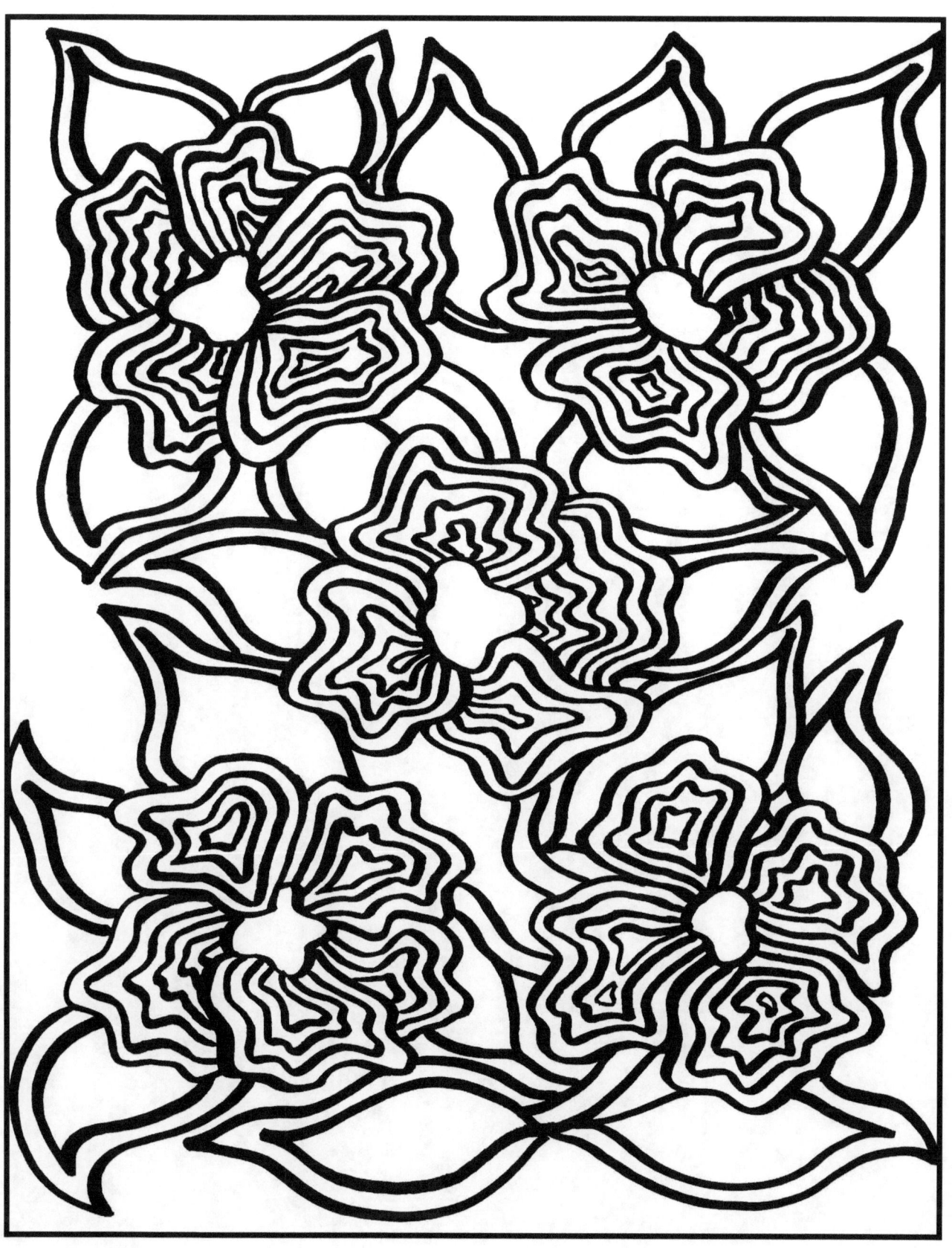

20

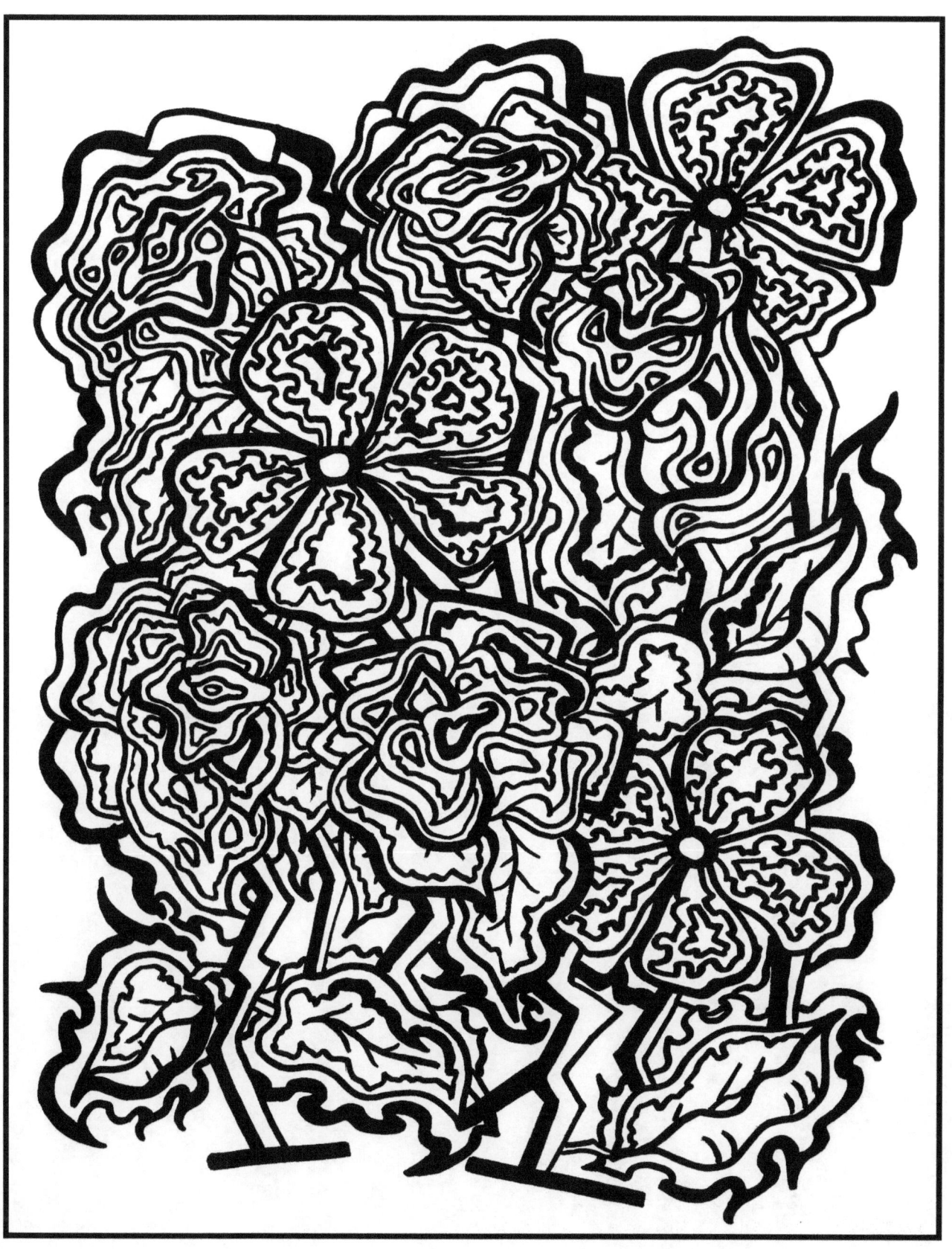

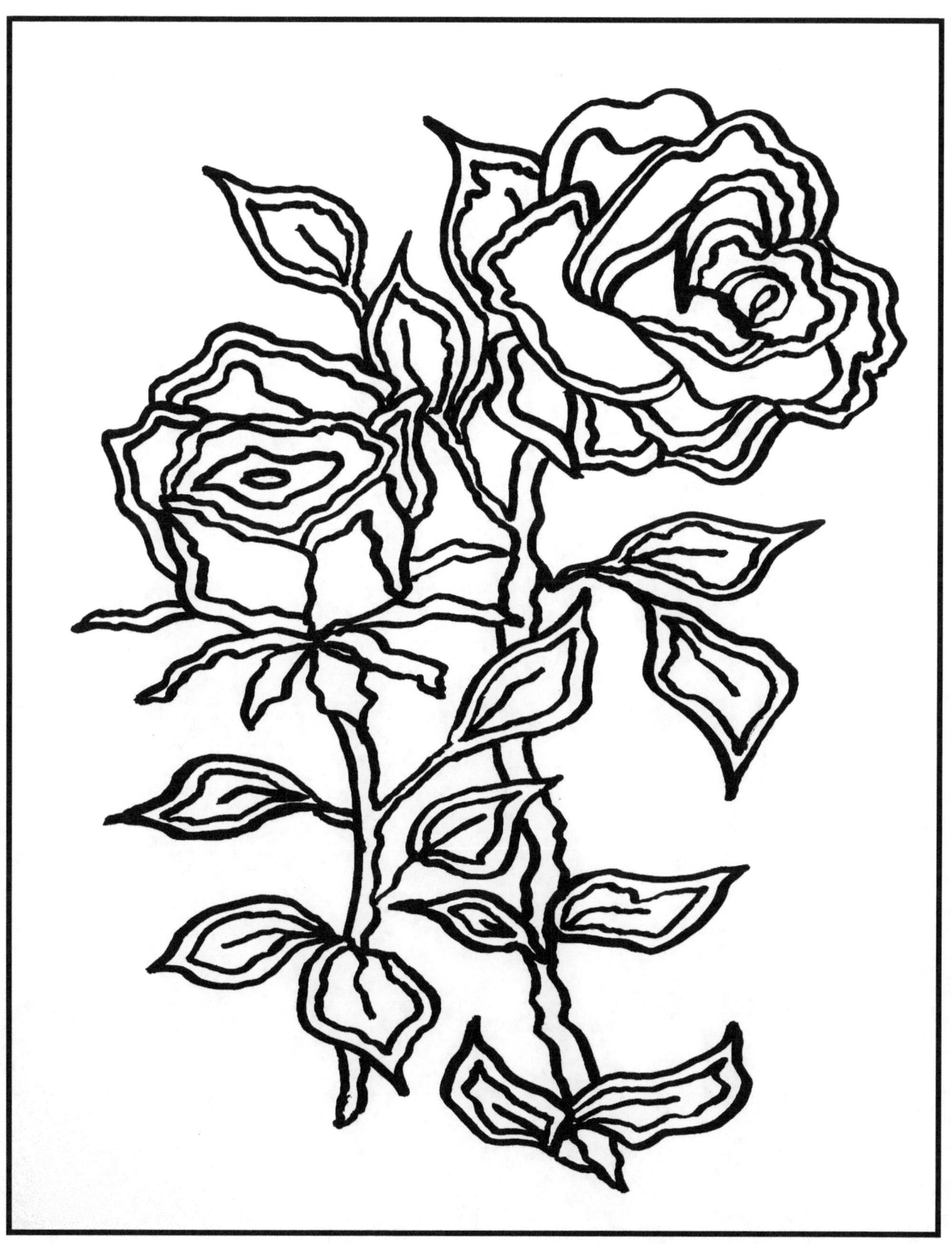

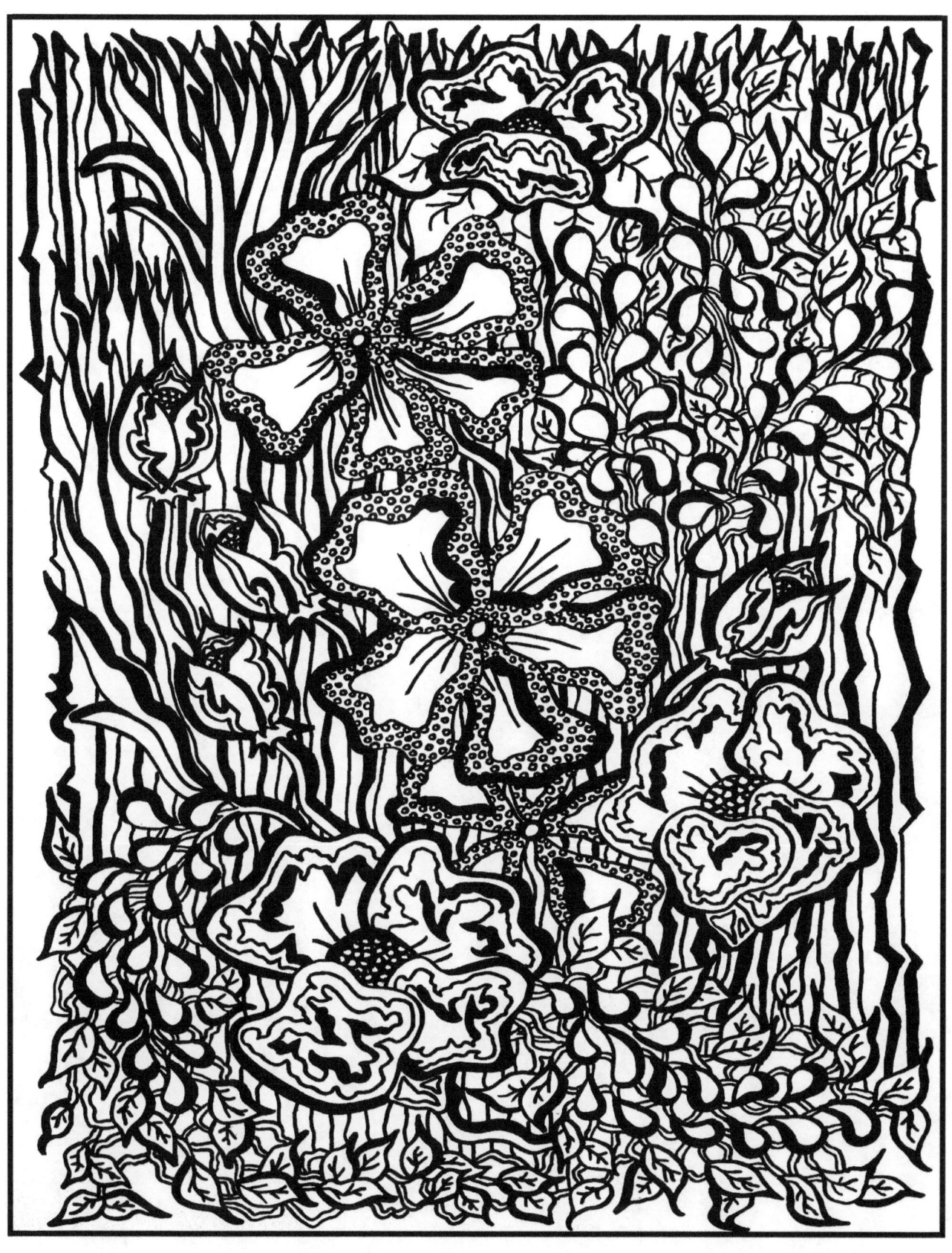

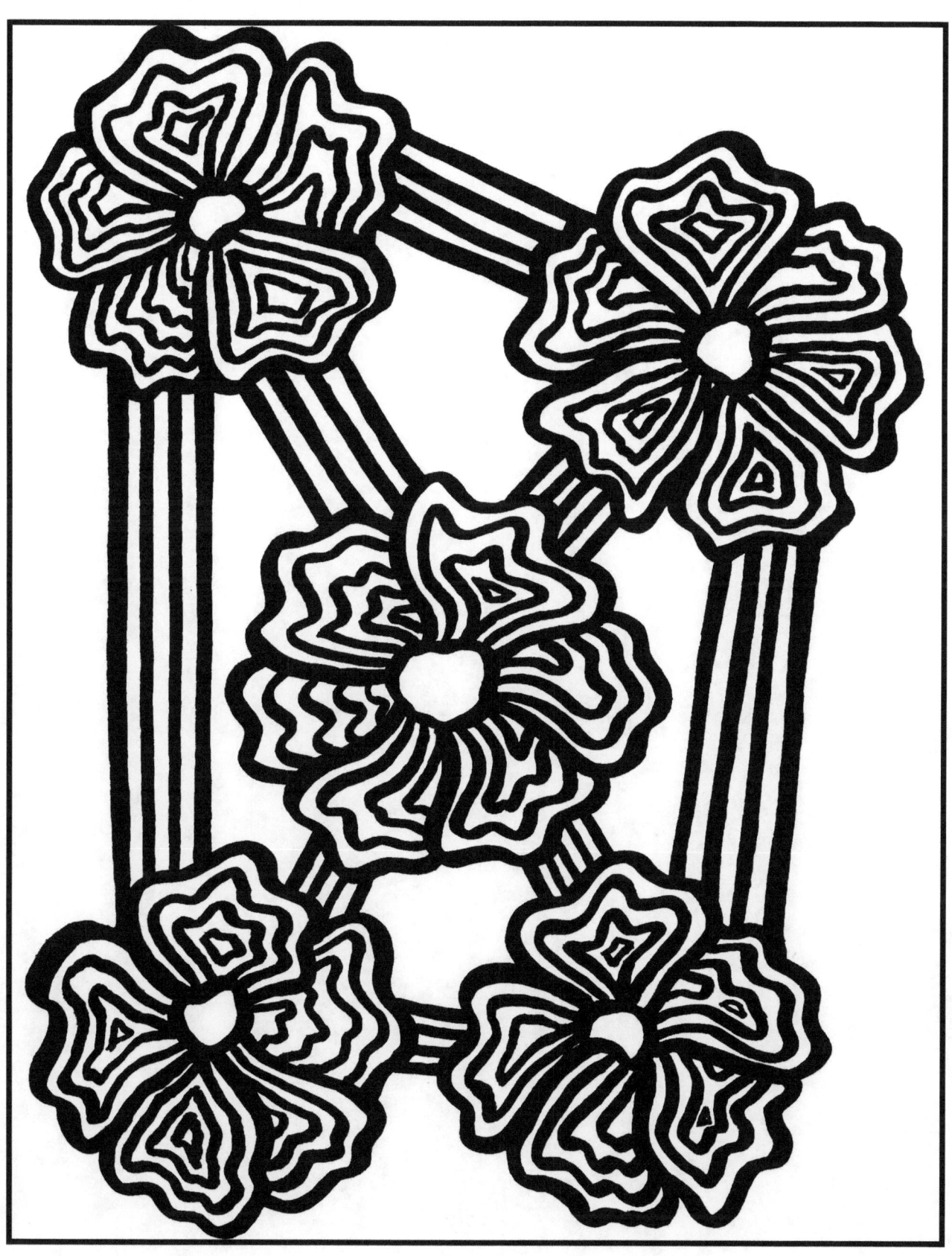

24

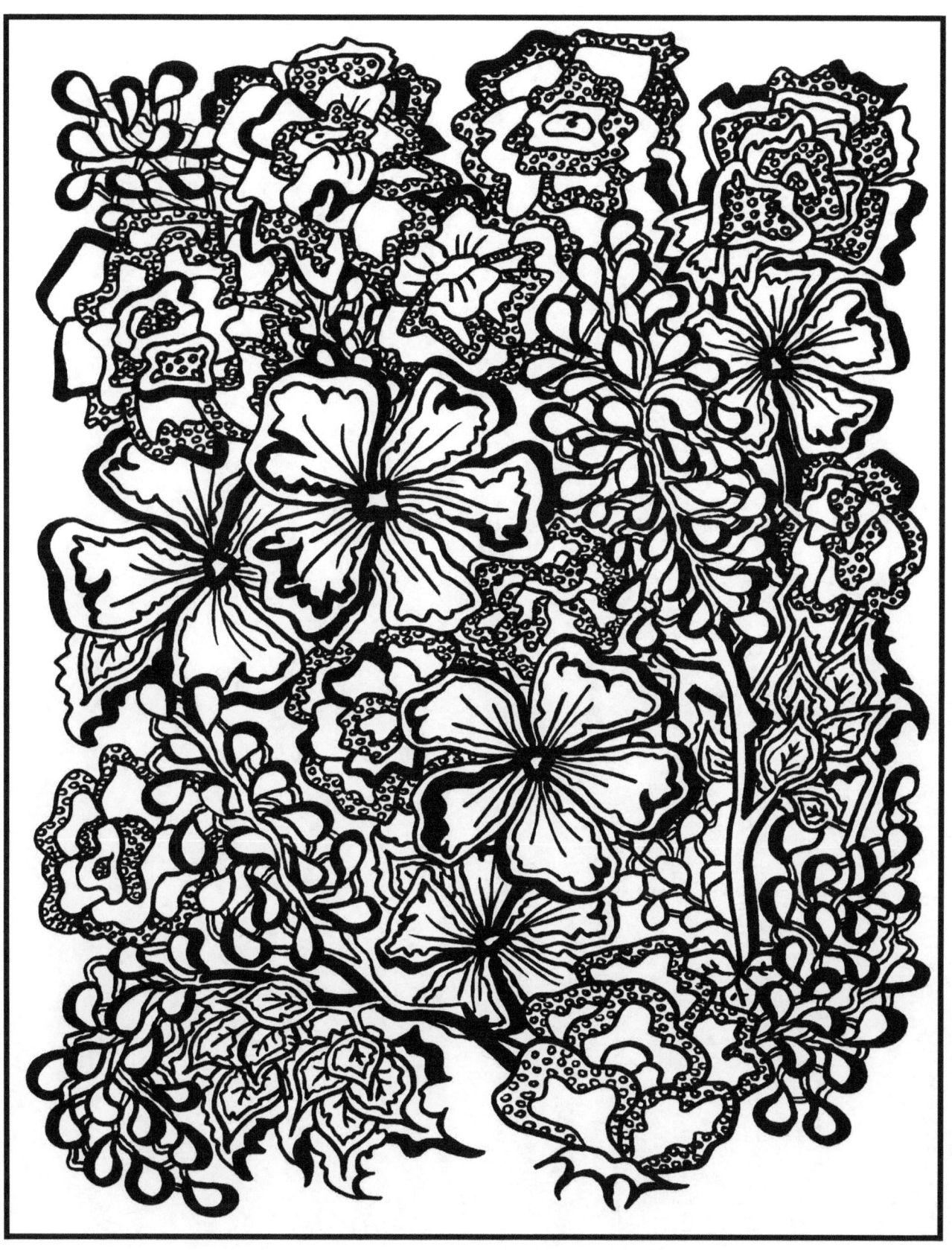

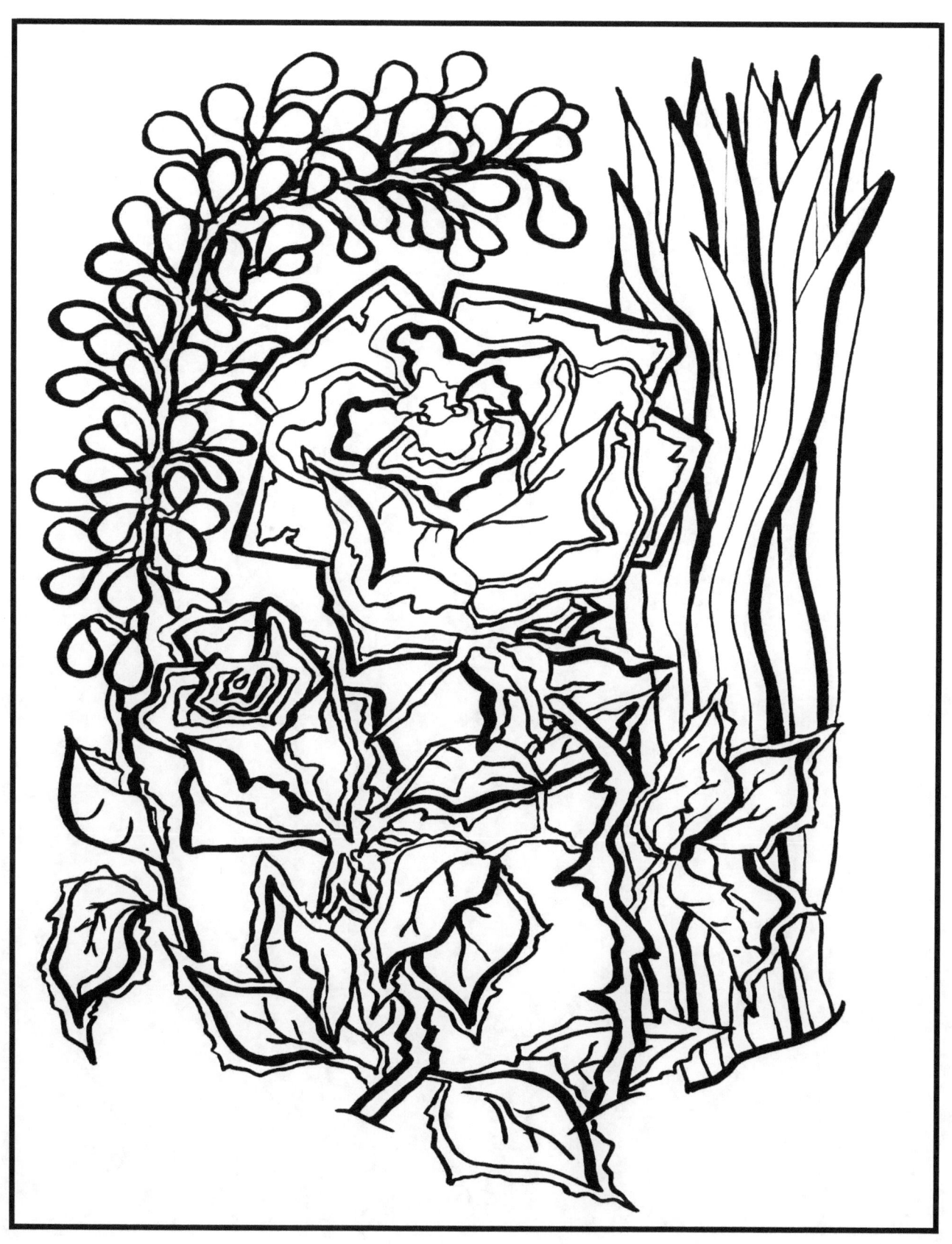

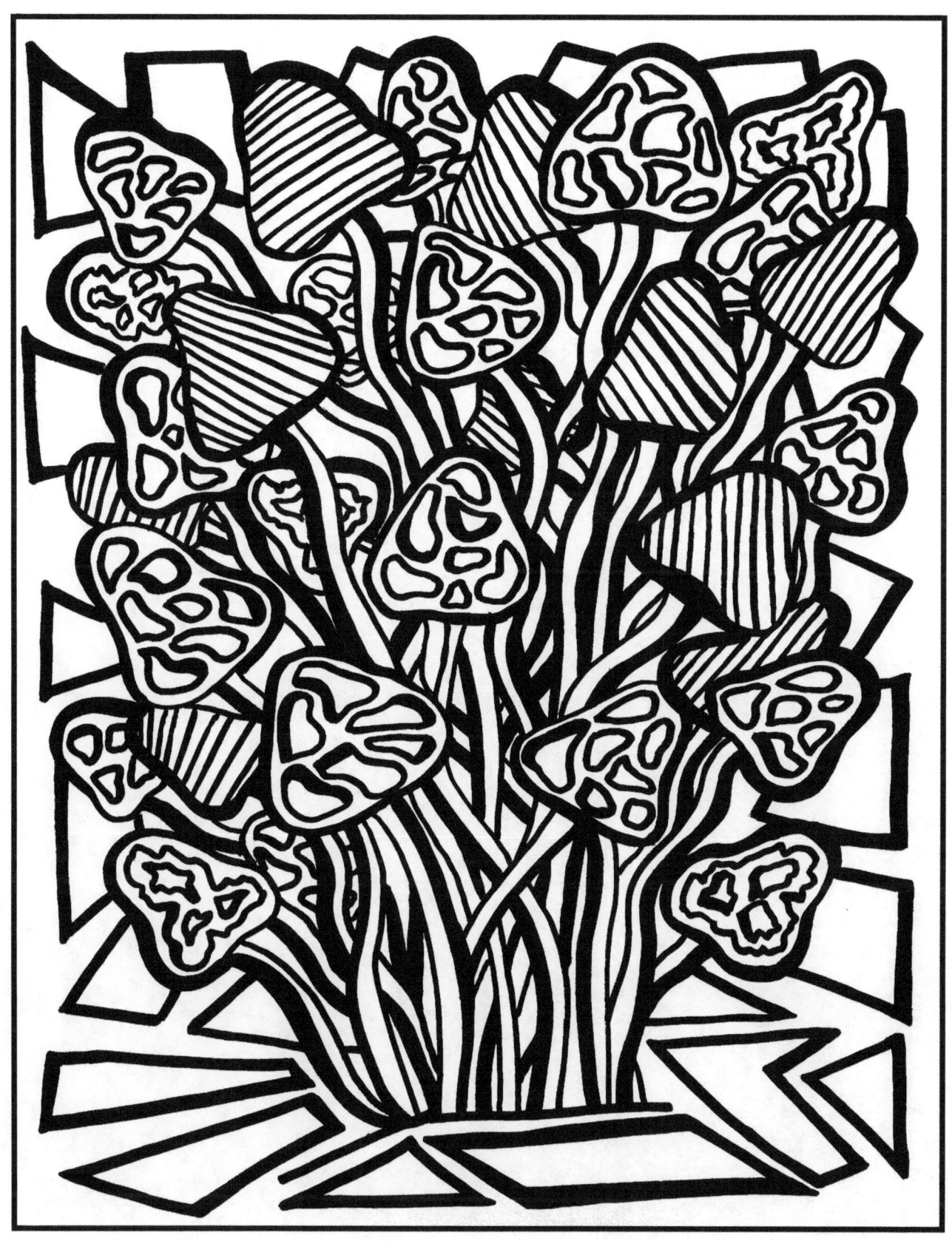

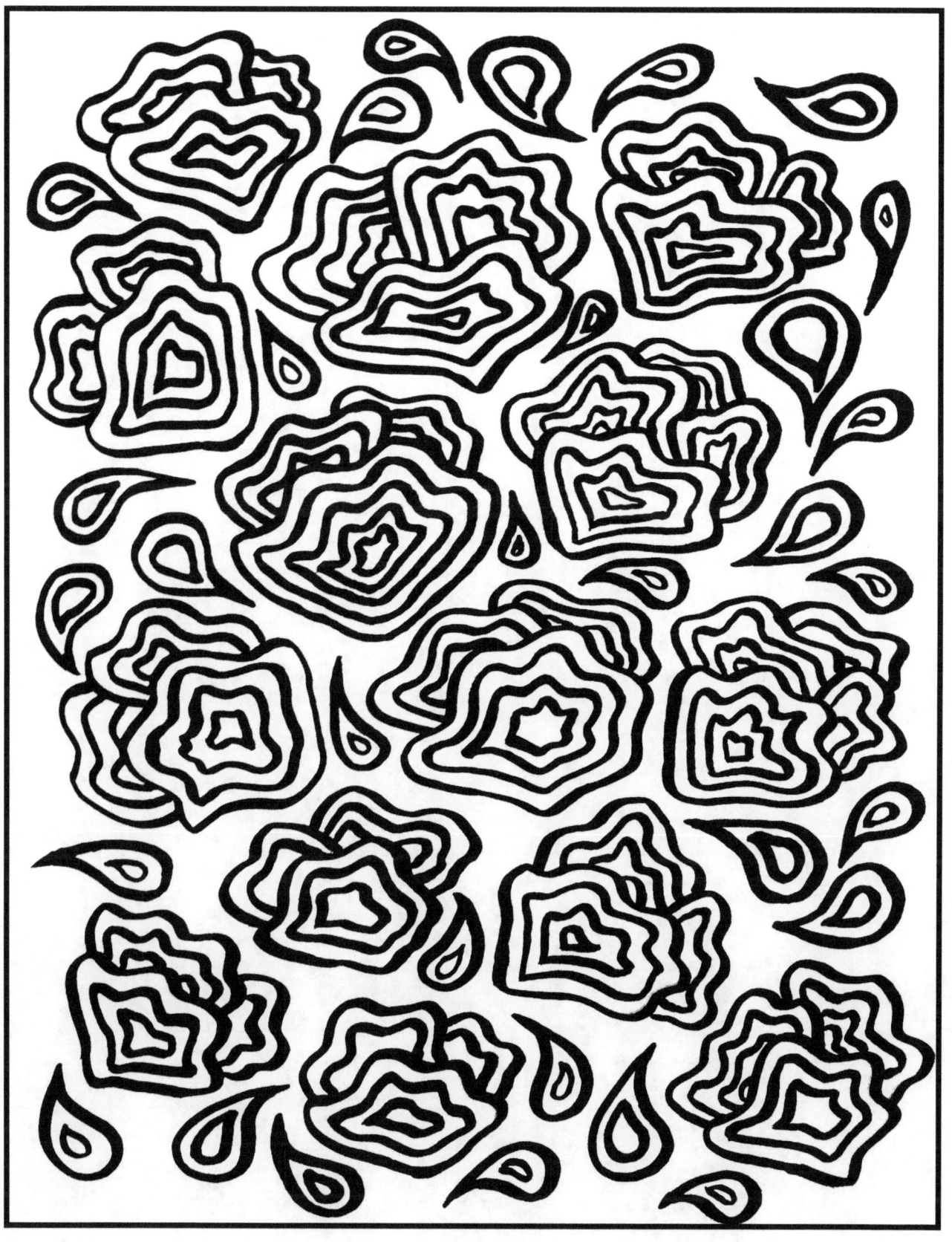

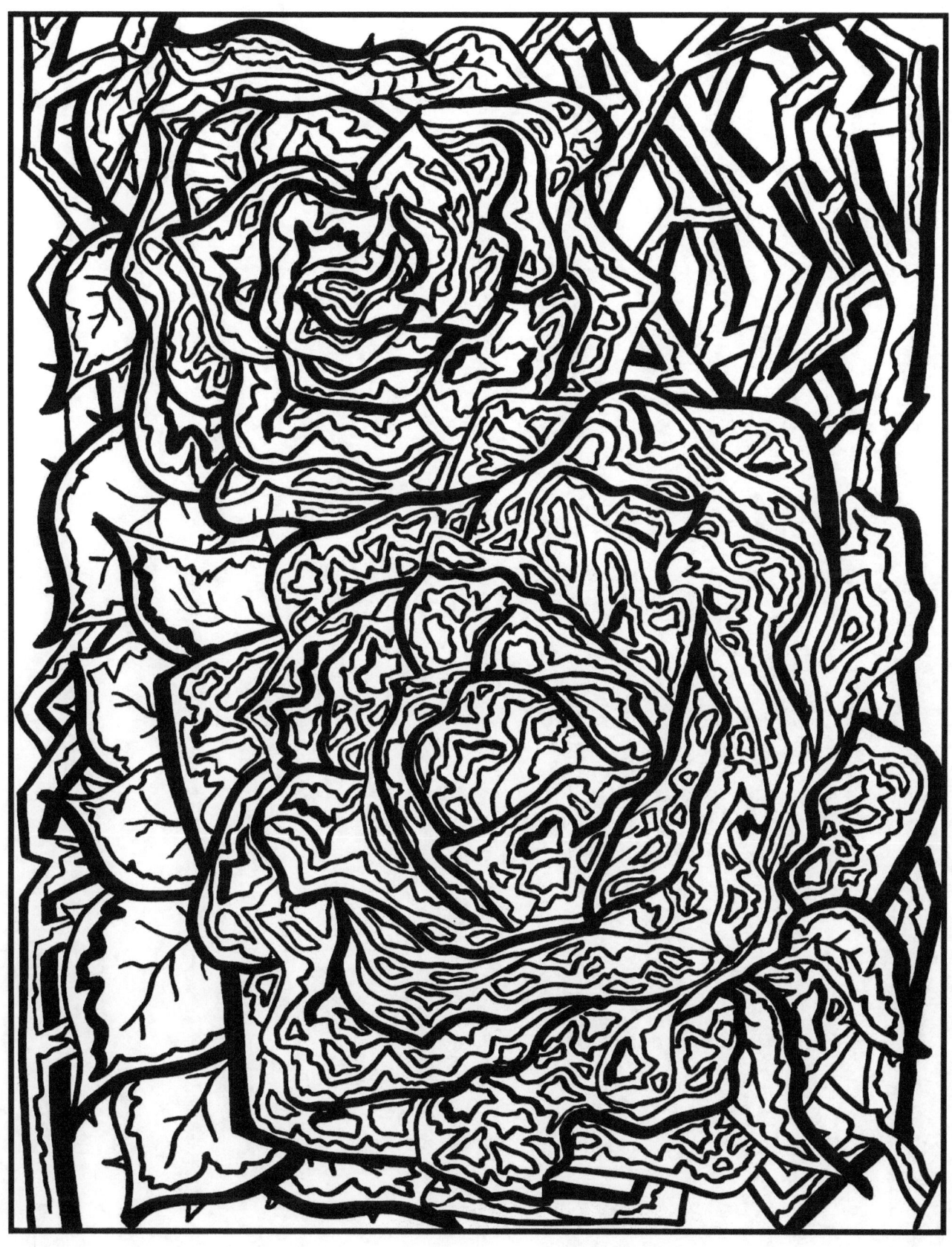

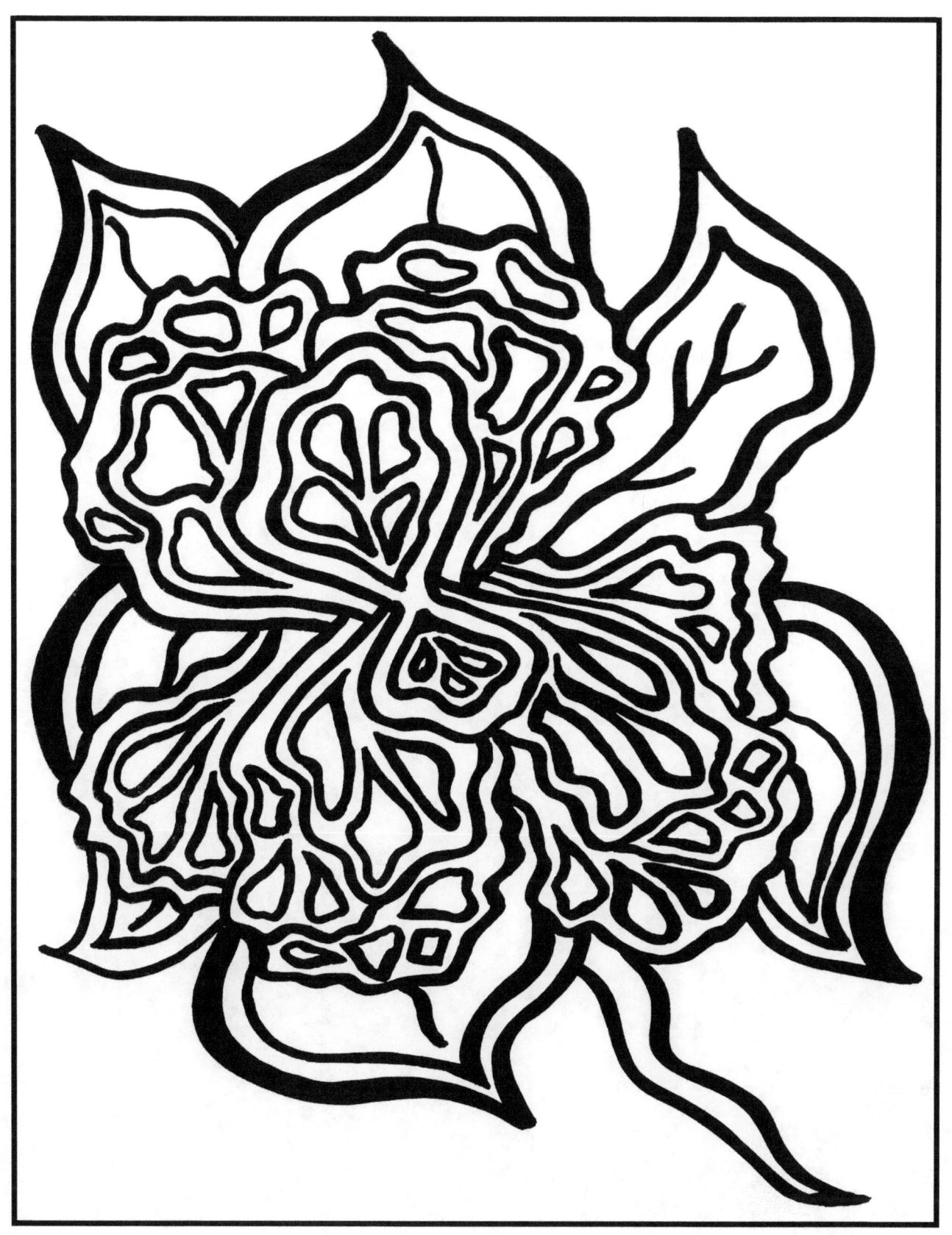

30

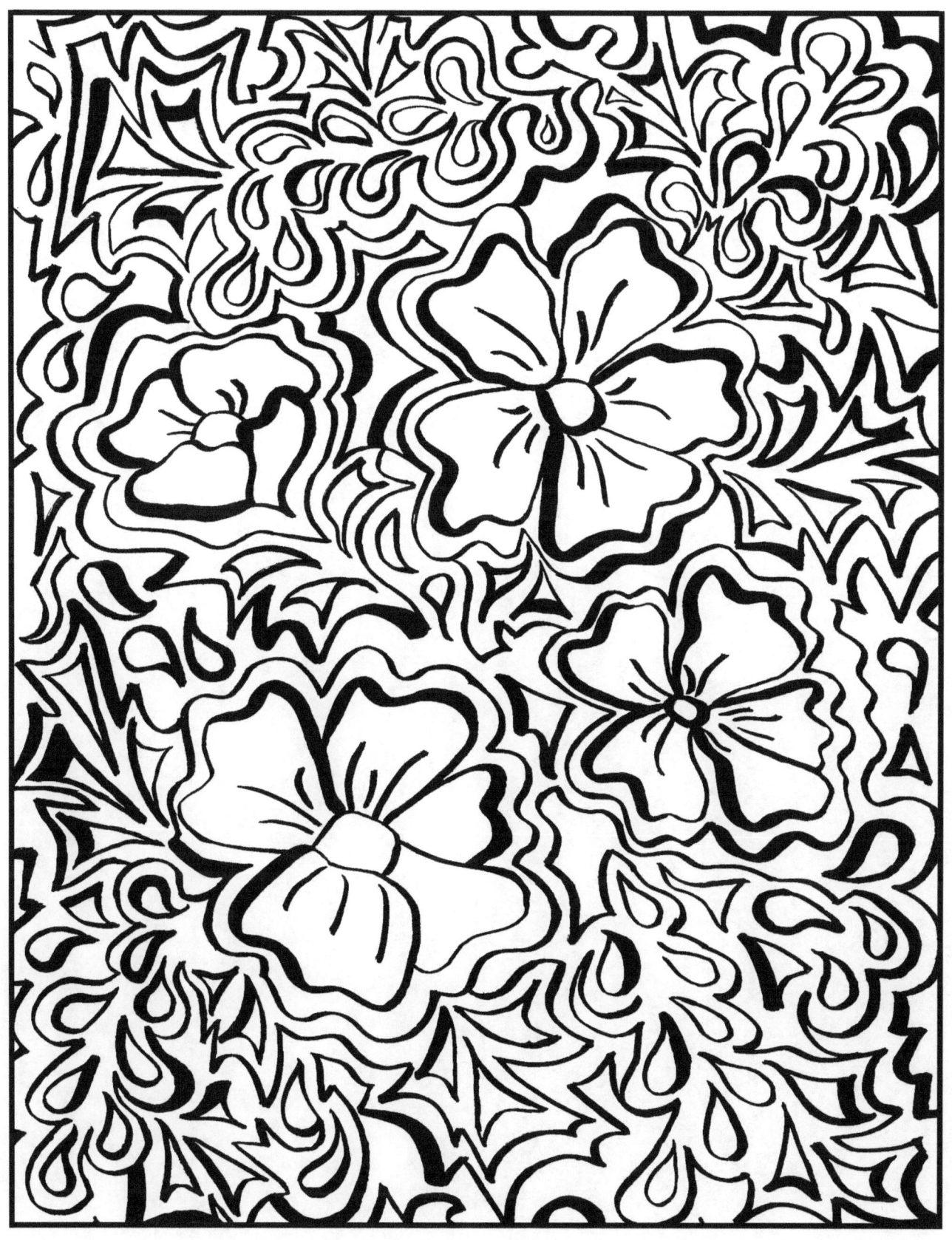

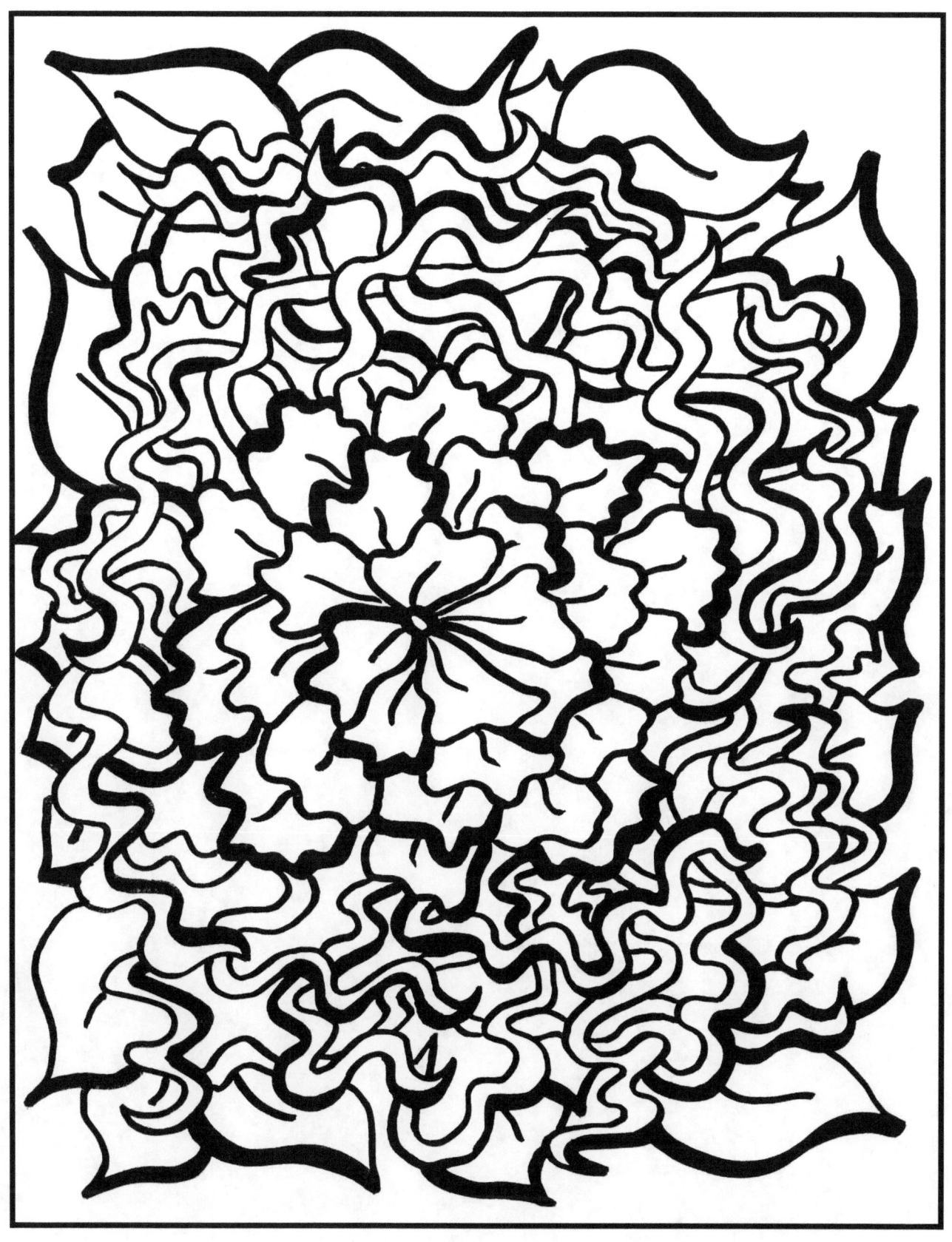

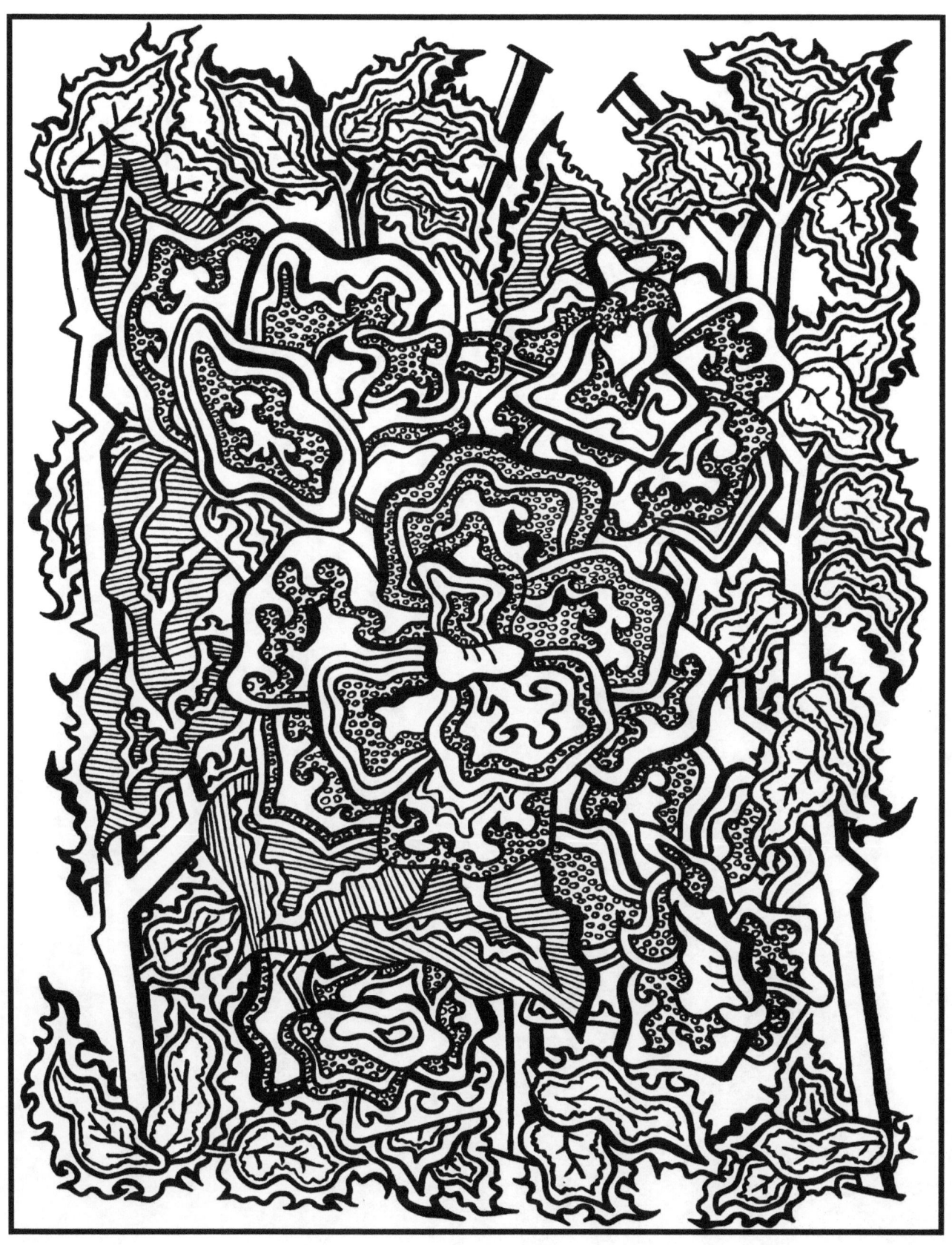

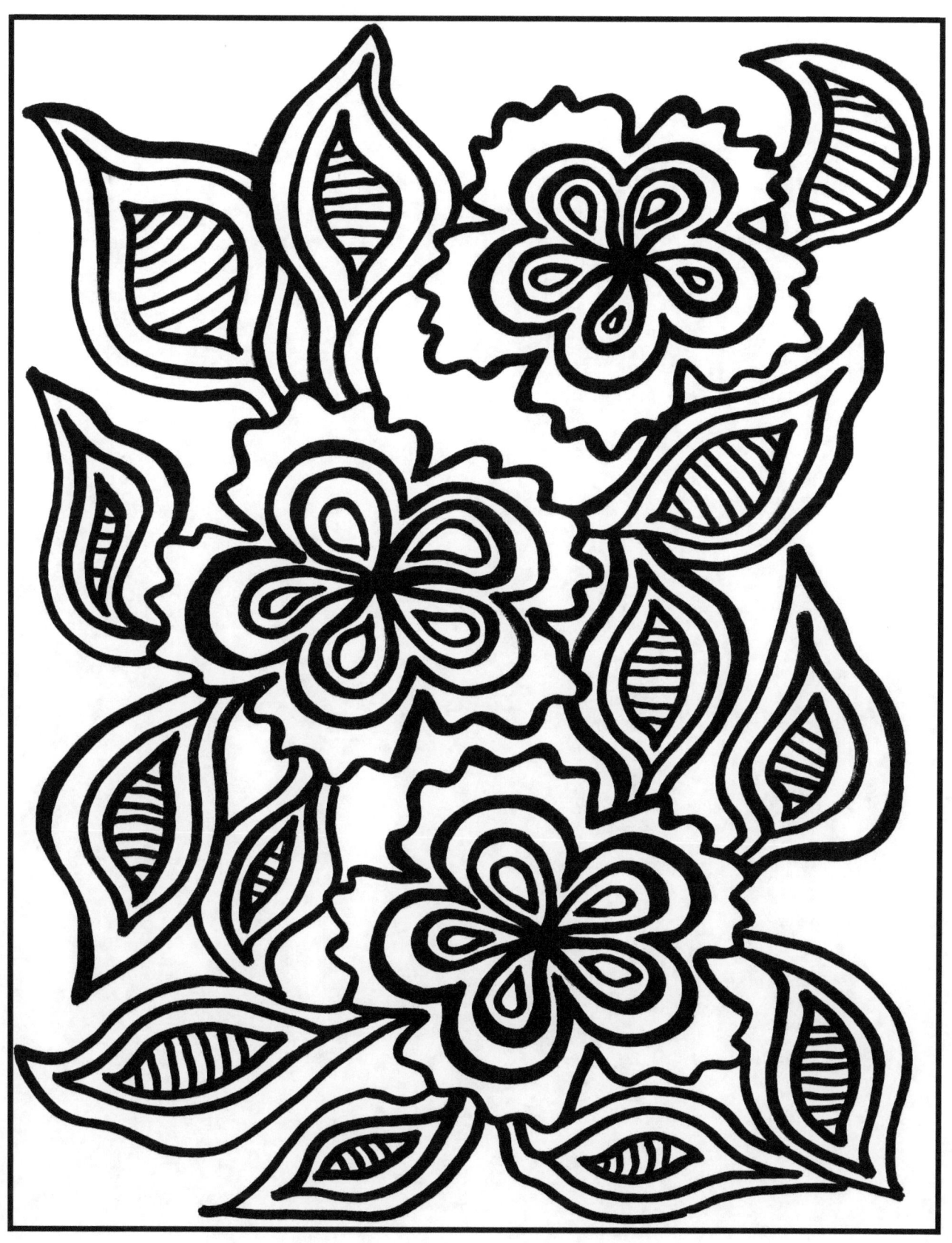

34

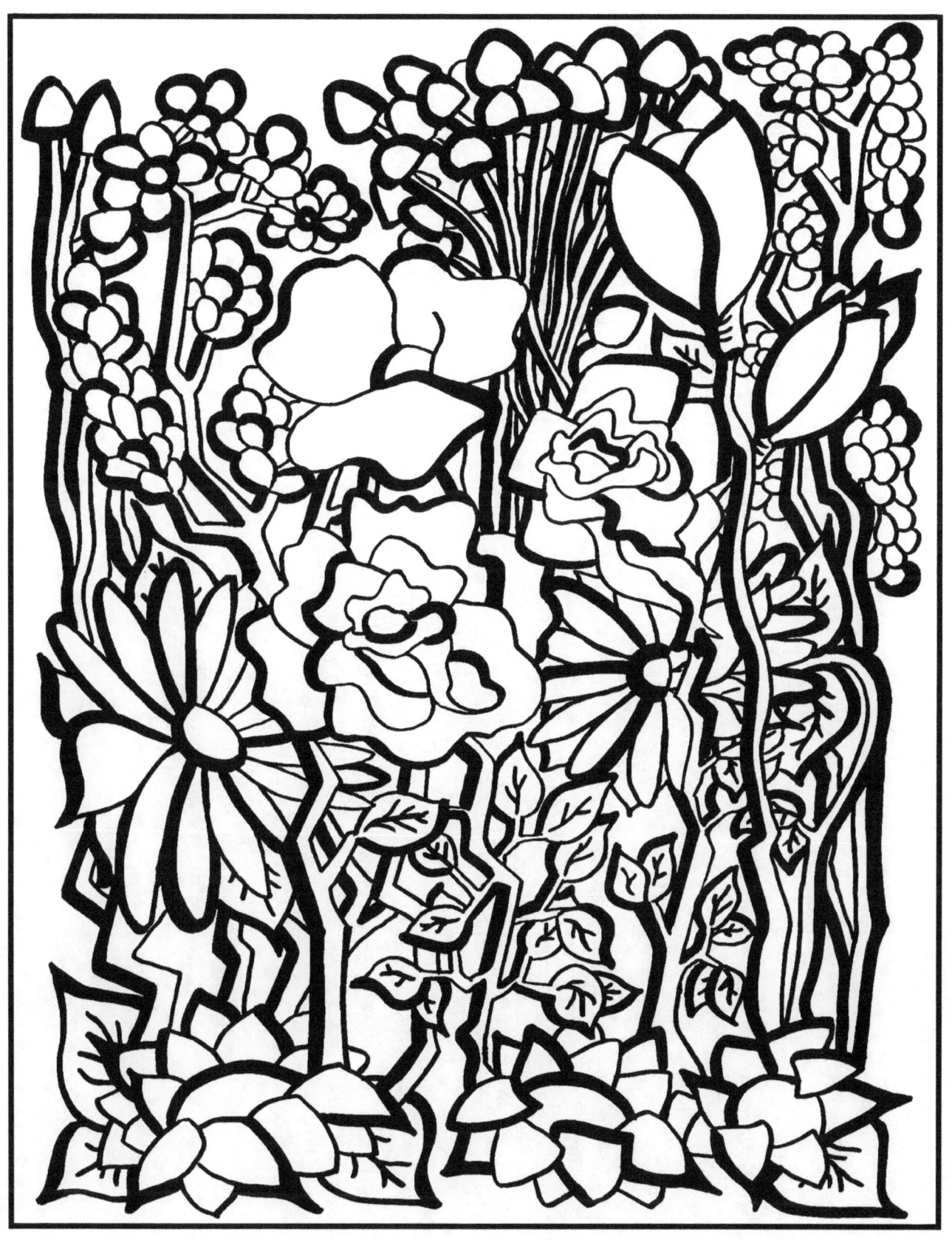

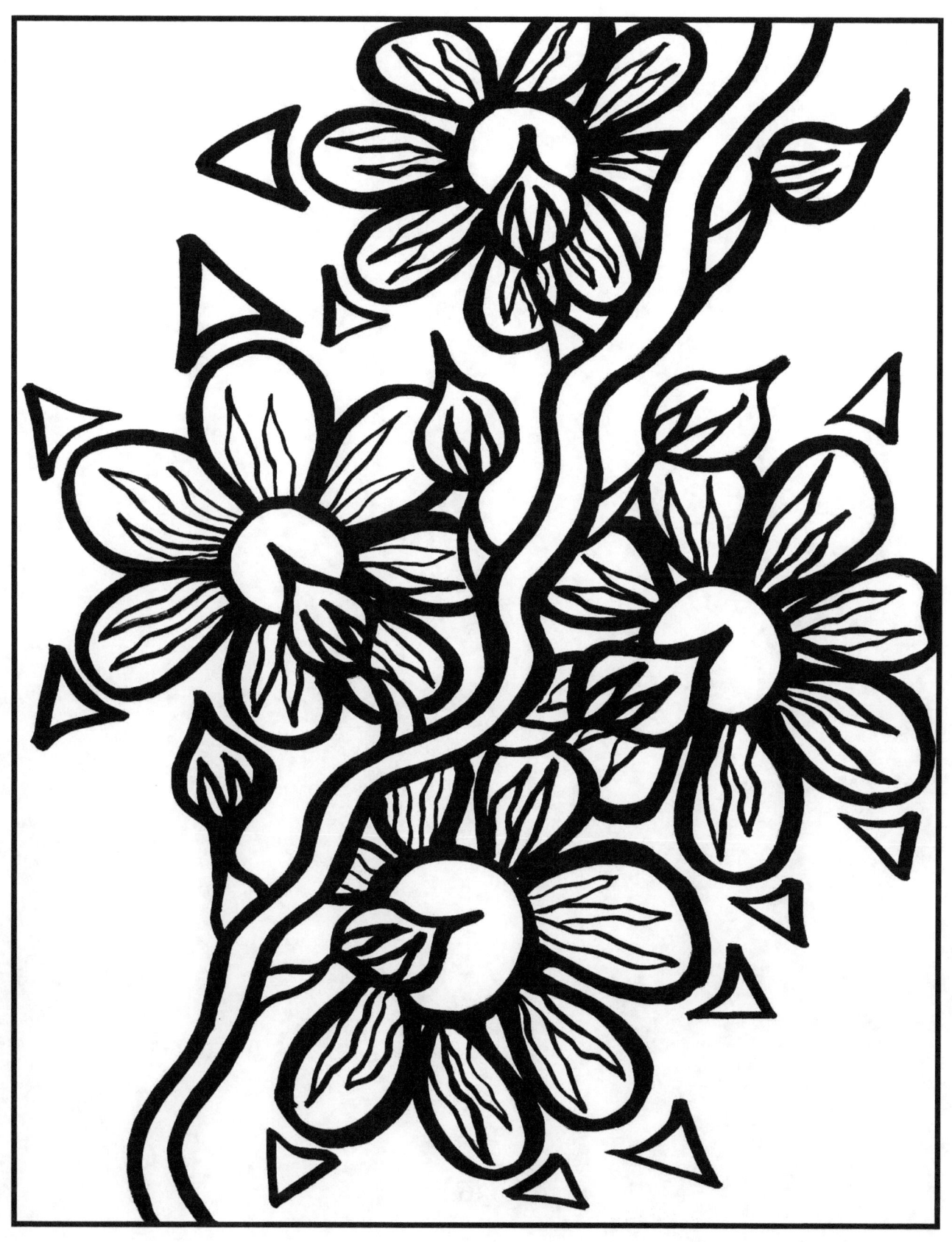

36

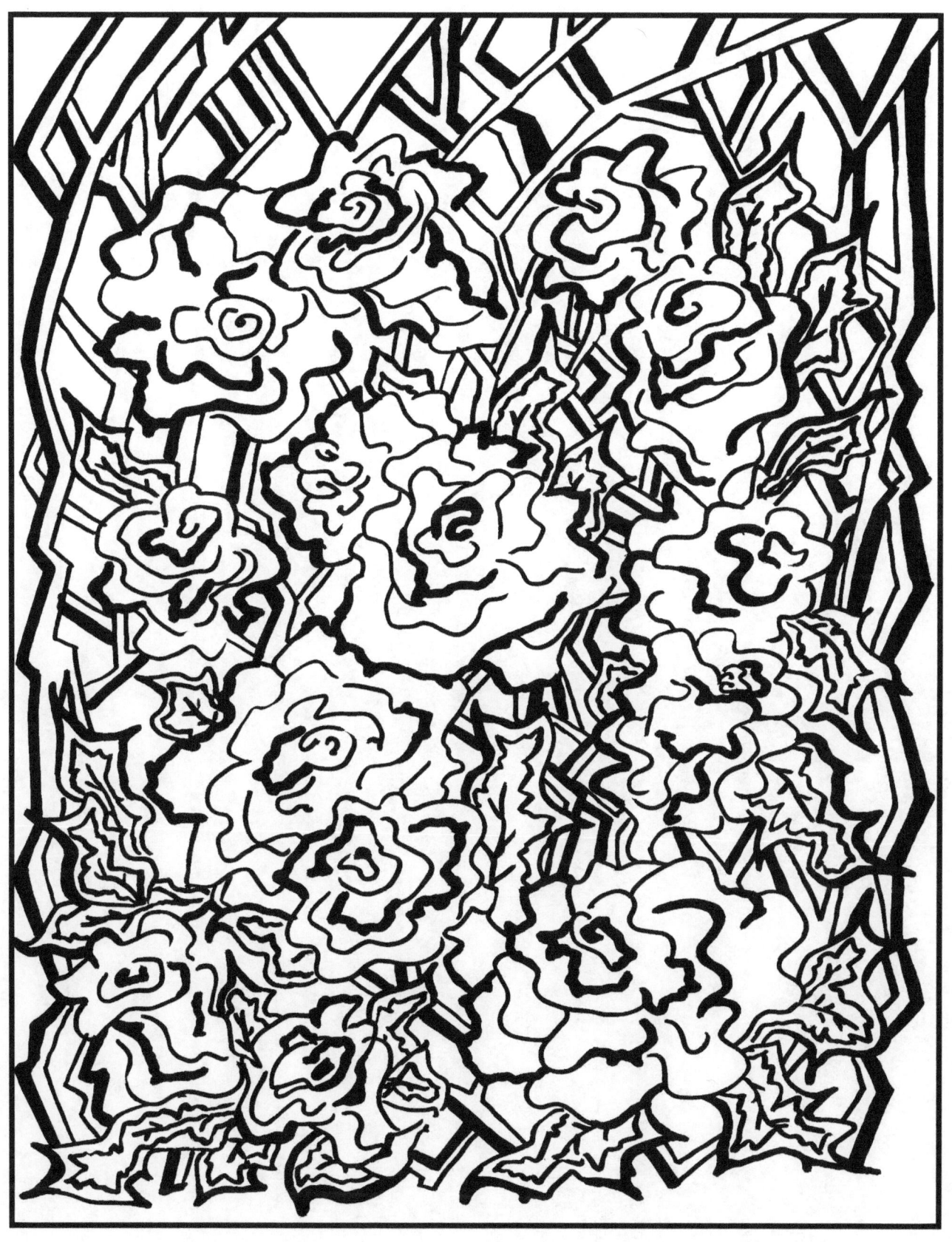

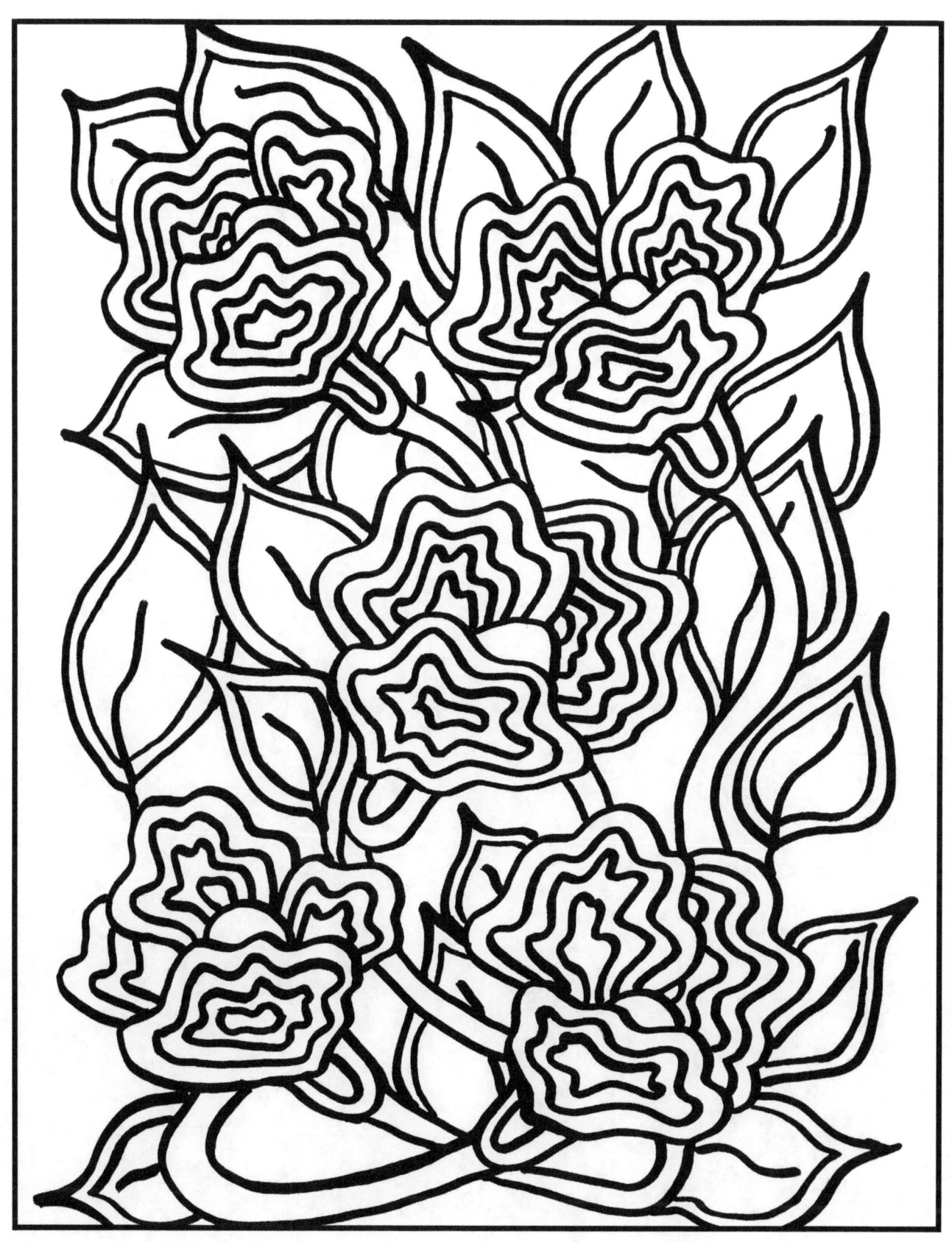

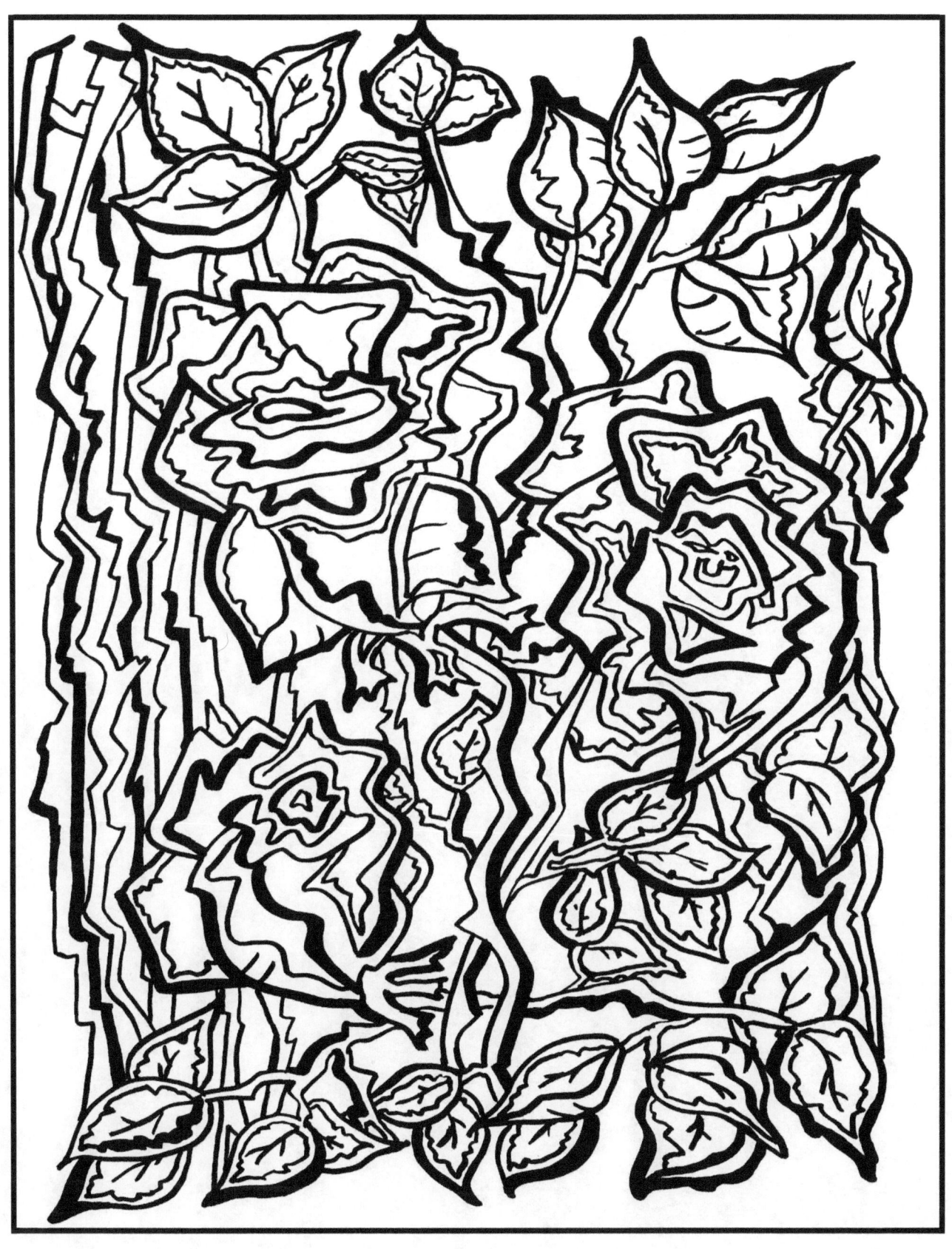

39

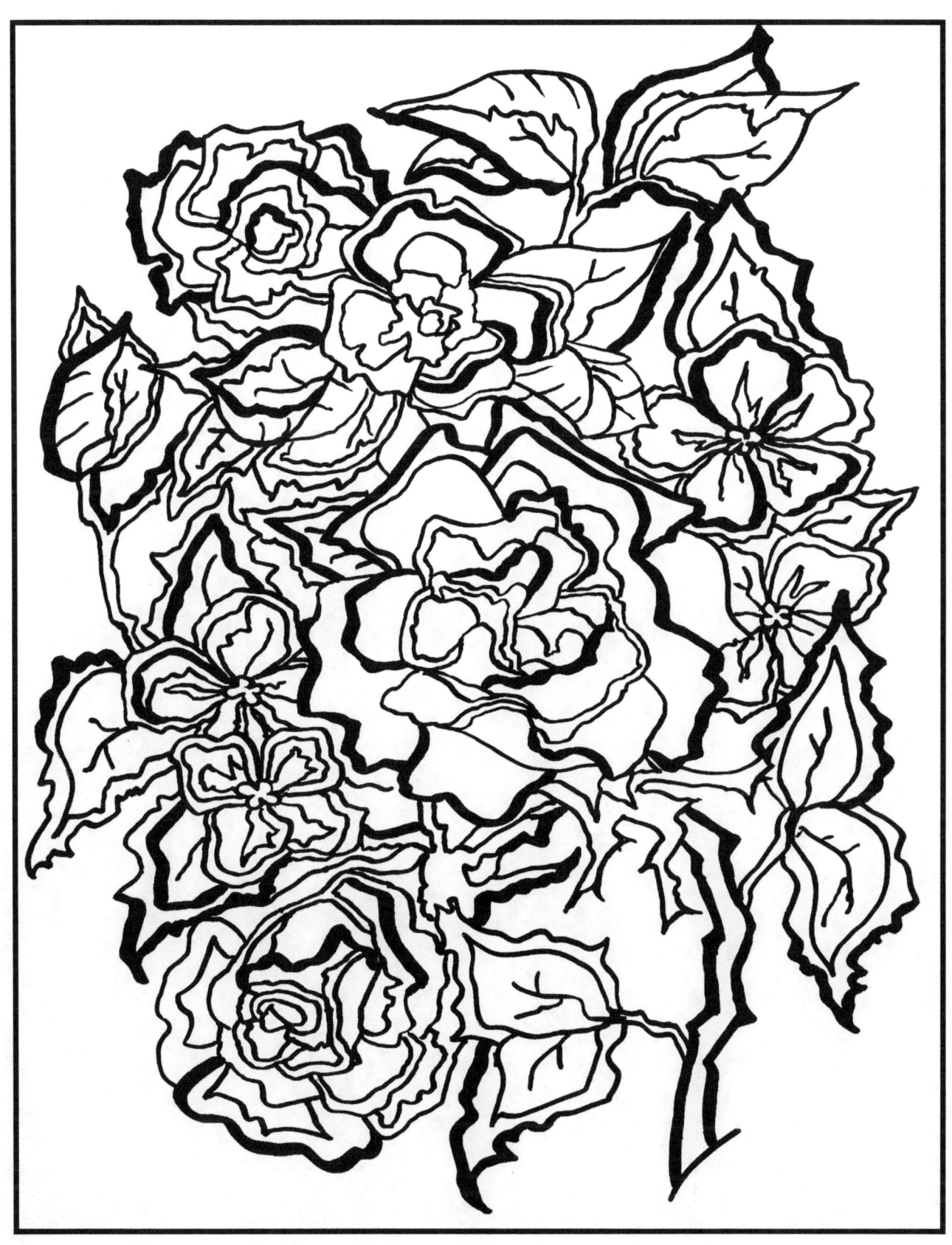

Media Test Page

Media Test Page

www.ingramcontent.com/pod-product-compliance
Lightning Source LLC
Chambersburg PA
CBHW080717190526
45169CB00006B/2417